22 24 26 28 30 32

North C

Söröy Hammerfest Porsangerfj rdö

Kvænangen Altaf Vadsö Varangerfj

Bossekop Kirkenes

FINNMARK

Karasjok

Kautokeino

Fishermens Peninsula

Murmansk

White Sea

Archangelsk

N S F

D

0 2 4 600 km

NORTH NORWAY

A HISTORY

K S Wilson
Bergen, 1959

Hvor dyrekjøbt er dette land
der sommerhavet vugger
med lyset fra soleigul strand
og kvite barnelugger.
Og sverm av sjofugl blir her nord
til luftens eget blomsterflor,
og nyskapt ligger haapets jord
i midnattsolens under.

NORDAHL GRIEG *Sang til Vardø*

TRANSLATION

A precious land, where summer stores
The ocean wave's caresses
With light from kingcup-golden shores
And children's flaxen tresses:
And countless seabirds weave on high
A garland for the arctic sky,
And midnight's magic sunbeams lie
On new-born hope's dominion.

G. M. GATHORNE-HARDY

NORTH NORWAY

A HISTORY

FRANK NOEL STAGG

WITH A FOREWORD BY
PROFESSOR A. H. WINSNES

LONDON
GEORGE ALLEN & UNWIN LTD
RUSKIN HOUSE · MUSEUM STREET

FIRST PUBLISHED IN 1952

PRINTED IN GREAT BRITAIN
in 12 point Fournier type
BY UNWIN BROTHERS LTD
WOKING AND LONDON

FOREWORD

FROM ancient times Northern Norway—the Land of the Midnight Sun—has appealed to men's imagination and to their spirit of adventure. As long ago as the fourth century B.C. Pytheas of Marseilles sailed northwards to *Ultima Thule* and today thousands of tourists follow where he and the other early voyagers led.

Northern Norway, however, has ceased to be solely a land of romance and adventure, for it has now been drawn into the currents of international affairs, and those who go north nowadays are no longer content merely to admire the magnificent scenery. They want to know, as well, something of the social and historical development of these parts and the role which they play in the affairs of Norway as a whole.

Hitherto this demand has not, to the best of my knowledge, been adequately met. Those who have been sufficiently interested to pursue the subject have usually been referred to scattered passages in specialised works of research, and Commander Stagg's book consequently fills a long-needed want. Norwegians and others alike will derive much benefit and pleasure from his instructive and delightfully written account, which abounds in interesting detail and is remarkable as much for the intimate knowledge it displays of past and present-day conditions as for the amount of information he has succeeded in compressing into a comparatively short space without sacrificing unity or interest.

Commander Stagg is animated by a deep affection for the peoples of the northern countries and is fully aware of the extent to which they share, with his own countrymen, the same ideals and beliefs. It is for this reason that he has devoted his life to strengthening and deepening a consciousness of the close bonds which unite the peoples on both sides of the North Sea.

It would be impossible, in the space of this brief foreword, to pay adequate tribute to what Commander Stagg has done in this field, but it would not be complete without at least a reference to the success which has attended his efforts and, above all, to the invaluable support he gave Norway's and Denmark's cause during the war. He was known, in those dark years, as 'the friend of Christmas Møller,' a title which has surely given him as much pleasure as the two high decorations bestowed on him by Norway and Denmark (the rank of Commander in the Order of St. Olav and in the Order of Dannebrog). And it will always be remembered that it was as a result of his initiative the moving Norwegian-Danish Memorial Service was held in Westminster Abbey on April 9, 1945.

The book about *North Norway* which Commander Stagg now has written agrees in the most beautiful way with the cause he has striven for all his life, the friendship and unity of the North Sea Powers.

A. H. WINSNES.

The University,
Oslo.

AUTHOR'S PREFACE

ON my travels up and down the coast of Nordland, Troms and Finnmark, sailing in their fjords, or motoring on the Great North Road (No. 50), I have so often felt keen regret that I knew literally nothing about the history of this most beautiful half of the Kingdom of Norway—'Det halve Kongerike.' My searches failed to bring to light any concise work in either of our languages detailing events in the past of North Norway.

I can but hope that this volume will increase the interest of citizens of many nations in the great traditions of the Land of the Midnight Sun.

My gratitude is due to the authors (both living and dead) of all the works mentioned in the Bibliography at the end of the volume. But I especially desire to thank Lektor Axel Coldevin, the local historian of Nordland Province, for his advice and corrections: also Dr. G. M. Gathorne-Hardy, who has permitted me to embody the result of his research into 'the Bodø Affair.' I am also most grateful to Messrs. Gunnar Berg and Harald Kaarbø for their interesting sidelights on the recent past of the Lofotens, and Lektors Erling Bjørgan of Vadsø, Ivar Lekang of Berlevaag and Mads Heie of Honningsvaag for their encouragement and assistance. Dosent Tore Sund of Bergen most kindly prepared the map at the ends of this volume.

It is, however, to Fredrik Wulfsberg—Cultural Attaché to the Royal Norwegian Embassy, London— that I am mainly indebted, since without his never-failing assistance this volume would not have appeared.

London, 1952.   FRANK NOEL STAGG.

CONTENTS

11

ILLUSTRATIONS

PART I

FROM THE ICE AGE TO
THE BATTLE OF STAMFORDBRIDGE
1066

THE last Ice Age left the west coast of Norway under the protection of a chain of islands and rocks that is almost continuous throughout its length of 1,000 miles. The channel within these islands is called 'The Inner Lead,' which has constituted Western Norway's 'Main Street' down the Ages.

In this sheltered channel there is one serious break where the Atlantic rollers surge in to Norway's mainland over a distance of some forty miles. This stretch of ocean is called Folla, and literally broke Norway in half in days when vessels were no more than crazy cockleshells, since no semblance of a road existed on the rugged mainland. Even in these times the passage of 'Folla' is so dreaded that many travellers prefer to use the railway, which was completed over this section as recently as 1940.

'Folla' lies between the 64th and 65th parallels of latitude and forms the southern boundary of North Norway, its northern being of course the frontier with Russia. Until quite recently North Norway was so divorced from the main southern portion that its history meets with but slight treatment in works of national history, and so it needs a volume to itself.

Place Names

From earliest times the four-hundred-mile stretch of coast between the 65th and 70th parallels of latitude (i.e. between Folla and Loppa) has been known as Haalogaland. Various interpretations are:

13

(*a*) 'The land of the tall and fair people'—given to distinguish them from the Samer (Lapps) who were short and dark.
(*b*) 'The land of the High Lights'—i.e. The Northern Lights.
(*c*) 'The holy land'—because it was the original home of all Norwegians.
(*d*) That it was named after the family of 'Earls'—the Haaløygjajarler—who exercised an overlordship during perhaps seven hundred years.

The most ancient place-names in all Norway are possibly those of several of the larger islands along this coast. Many are so old as to defy interpretation without the aid of other Germanic tongues, whilst some are beyond elucidation.

Fjord-names such as Vefsnir (Vefsn), Radund (Rana), Bedi (Beiarn), Saltpi (Salten), Ofoti (Ofoten), Bagangr (Ballangen) and others go back to prehistoric times, whilst those ending in -angen, such as Gratangen, date from a remote era.

The oldest *farm*-names are combined with '-vin,' which is used both as a termination and independently in names of old farms in Haalogaland. Vinje on Dyrøya, Venset in Skjerstad, and as a final syllable in Bodin.

Somewhat later than -vin names are those which terminate in '-heimr' (dwelling-place). From the Viking period date names ending in -stadir (now 'stad') of which there are one hundred in Haalogaland. From the same period come names ending in '-land,' and somewhat later the ending 'setr.' The '-rud' (in North Norway the usual form is 'rød') names recall pioneering in mediaeval times.

But by far the greatest number of names in the North have local roots based on the characteristics of the countryside, such as -vik, vaag, fjord, sund, nes, berg, sand and sjø—many of which go far back in time.

Classical References to North Norway

Greece and Rome must have known a little about North Norway, since *Homer*—who lived three thousand years ago—mentions in his Odyssey a land where there was no night.

Herodotus—who wrote in 450 B.C.—had heard of a people far in the north who slept for six months in the year.

14

Pytheas of Marseilles (330 B.C.) actually made a voyage to North Europe at the time of Alexander the Great. Pytheas was an astronomer and geographer who was the first to connect the ebb and flow of the tide with the antics of the moon. One spring he sailed round Gibraltar to the north in search of tin and amber. He must have gone to Scotland since he talks of the longest day being eighteen hours, and it was no doubt in the Shetlands that he heard of a land with light summer nights where the sun never set. Although the summer was far advanced he sailed across the unknown sea for six days when he reached a land he calls 'Thule,' where the sun did not set at Midsummer. He must himself have seen the Midnight Sun, since in a later description of his journey he says he saw a section of the sun above the horizon at midnight.

It is not known how far north Pytheas travelled, but he was certainly in a high latitude in the autumn and probably spent the winter there. That he should have sailed from Scotland to Norway on a known course is proof that the country of Norway, and voyages across the North Sea, were known in Scotland as early as 330 B.C.

Pytheas was amazed to see corn being threshed inside the houses, whilst he records that instead of wine the people drank a mixture of corn and honey—a kind of mead.

Latin writers around A.D. 100 make references to what is surely Norway, and mention 'Dumna' which is possibly the modern *Dønna* in Helgeland (66°).

Jordanes who lived in A.D. 550 and wrote the history of the Goths, mentions a people in Scandinavia called Adogit as inhabiting the most northern part of the country. Some authorities believe this to be intended for 'Andogi,' the people of Andøya (69°), whilst others think it refers to 'Alogii,' the people of Haalogaland.

Procopios, the famous Byzantine historian who also lived around A.D. 550, described life and customs among the ancient northerners. He records that the sun does not set in Thula during the summer solstice, when it is visible uninterruptedly for forty days, whilst there is darkness for the same period during the winter solstice. He states that when thirty-five days of darkness have been counted a party of men climb to the mountain-tops, and when they sight the rim of the sun they warn the people below that in five days they will get their first glimpse of sunlight. Thereupon a great feast was prepared, and it is thus that Procopios described 'Yule' among the people of Haalogaland in the year A.D. 500.

Rock-Carvings

The most ancient rock-carvings—'hellerristninger'—in all Northern Europe are found in North Norway. North of 'Folla' there are no more than fourteen, but they are the most interesting of all the 1,000 or more rock-carvings in Norway. Five of them belong to the Early Stone Age (before 3000 B.C.), the most ancient being at the head of Sagfjord on Hamarøy (68°), being probably 8,000 years old. It portrays two reindeer masterfully drawn, following each other with bowed heads as though biting moss or drinking. It now lies 150 ft. above sea-level—by so much has the land risen during 8,000 years.

At Leiknes on Tysfjord (68°) there are cuttings of about forty figures—elk, reindeer, bear, a large whale, fish and birds, also a tiny animal that is believed to be a hare. It is thought that the red Stone Age dye still persists on this carving.

The earliest of these Stone Age carvings are cut into the rock with a hard stone, sand and water, whilst the later 'hellerristninger' are carved with a sharp tool. They all picture the hunted quarry on mountain or in fjord, the cult of the hunter being linked up with magic. Some archaeologists believe these places were used as assembly-points for the hunting folk who cut these figures at certain seasons and with special ceremonies.

Artistically these North Norway carvings are of a high order being far superior to those farther south. Animal figures are cut into the rock with a sure eye and are almost lifelike. It is a primitive art that tells us not a little about our ancestors, and of their struggle for existence with nature at its severest.

1. Bronze sacrificial cauldron found at Bjarkøy—
from *c.* A.D. 500

2. The oldest rock-carving in Norway,
at Sagfjord on Hammarøy

The Early Stone Age (before 3000 B.C.)

Who and what were these ancient men of the Stone Age? The Saga-writers believed that Norway was first populated by migration from the north via the White Sea. This theory was accepted by historians of the early nineteenth century, and Ivar Aasen made his first trip to Helgeland in 1846 in order to investigate it.

But we have had to wait until 1925 to obtain some tangible indications of this migration from the north, in the discoveries of Dr. Nummedal, who has made more than seventy 'finds' in Finnmark during the past twenty-five years. It was on the promontory of Komsa by Bossekop (70°) that Nummedal made his first discovery, and so it has been called the 'Komsa Culture.' These very early Stone Age settlements lie at the heads of fjords or at their seaward entrances, and at Karlebotn (70°) a considerable Stone Age 'town' of seventy-two houses was found.

Behind these primitive people lay the glaciers and before them the pack-ice, as in the northern areas of the Arctic Ocean today. This lends support for the theories of Professor Nordhagen that the shores of Finnmark were ice-free during the long last Ice Age, and there was nothing to prevent Stone Age man wintering there, just as on Greenland and similar polar areas today.

This Komsa Culture shows affinity with archaeological finds in Siberia, North China, the arctic shores of North America and even Greenland. There is also similarity with the finds in more southerly Nordland, but these—known as Fosna Culture—do not go back so far in time.

The Later Stone Age (3000–1500 B.C.)

From this period only two settlements have been found in Troms Province, but many exist along the coast of Nordland—especially at Rødøy ($65\frac{1}{2}$°) where cultures similar to those of Komsa-Fosna have left remains at 120–150 ft. above sea-level.

At Meløy (67°) was found the beautiful 'Risvik' knife with a finely modelled head of an elk on the shaft.

The Bronze Age (1500–500 B.C.)

This has yielded only five finds so far in Nordland and one in Troms Province—at Tennevik in Skaanland ($68\frac{1}{2}°$)—the most northerly Bronze Age find in all Norway. Some authorities believe that Stone Age drifted into Iron Age up here without an intermediate bronze, and others think there was a 'bone age' in between. Stone and iron implements are found in the same graves and of the same period.

The Iron Age (500 B.C.–A.D. 1050)

This lasted long in Norway and is divided into two main parts—the 'early' between 500 B.C. and A.D. 800, whilst the 'later' covers the Viking Age from A.D. 800–1050.

The influence of Roman Culture penetrated up to the far north, but the Norsemen did not slavishly copy the Roman work and models—they created an independent Norwegian Culture. Finds are particularly rich in the outer districts of Vesteraalen where—near Bø (69°)—are about two hundred barrows in two groups, the largest burial-place in Vesteraalen.

The small uninhabited islands along the coast were used as cemeteries as far back as the Roman Iron Age (before A.D. 400).

From the *Migration Period* (A.D. 400–600) a number of finds have been made, including the *bronze cauldron* of Frankish form which was found on Bjarkøy (69°) in 1894, that is without question the largest of its kind known in Northern Europe. It was certainly a sacrificial cauldron from the fifth century and can now be seen in the Historical Museum at Oslo.

From the *Merovingian* Period (A.D. 600–800) graves of women have been found, and much therein shows that women were on an equality with men. Many monoliths date from these centuries around which are woven mythical stories.

Haalogaland had a fairly densely settled population during the Viking Period (A.D. 800–1050), and a female grave at Ekkerøy (70°) in Varanger from early tenth century contained a rich supply of Norwegian and Finno-Baltic ornaments of silver and bronze.

18

Haalogaland Prior to the Foundation of the Kingdom of Norway in 872

We have to glean what we can from the Sagas—mainly from the *Haaløygjatal*. This was composed in about A.D. 985 by the last and greatest of Norwegian skalds (himself a Haalogalander) Øjvind Skaldespiller, with the object of glorifying the family of the 'Earls of Haalogaland.'

The centres of economic and political life in Haalogaland lay along the 'Inner Lead' at the points of junction where fjords cut across, or where fishing conditions were favourable. At each of these centres a 'plutocrat' family established itself, whose head was the petty chieftain over an area as large as he could acquire and control. Each of these 'plutocrats' would have been a law unto himself in his own domains, and any higher authority did not exist. But it would seem that in times of general trouble there must have been some 'plutocrat' who was looked upon as leader, and the Sagas cause one to guess that it was the 'Earl' of Haalogaland. This family were plutocrats in the district of *Aamd* (later Omd), their ancient headquarters being near Andenes (69¼°).

Aamd is now called *Vesteraalen*, and here is not only the best farming soil in all Haalogaland, but the ocean fishing banks lie close into the coast. Moreover its shores are well protected from all points of the compass by narrow 'sounds' that could easily be held against an enemy afloat. It was also an ideal point of departure for expeditions to procure furs, etc., in modern Finnmark and Murmansk, and to hunt and fish the valuable products of the Arctic Ocean.

Saga-legends make it a probability that a petty king named *Godest* ruled here in about the sixth century, and that he was killed riding a horse named Rafn which had been presented to him by King Adils of Uppsala. A tiny stream on Andøy named Ramsaa is said to commemorate that of the horse which killed his master here. Verbal traditions preserved this tale—perhaps because Godest was the progenitor of the famous family of 'Haaløygjajarler.'

A later king of Aamd named *Gudlaug* loaded a vessel with valuables and set sail to do some trading in Denmark—no doubt to barter furs, eiderdown and walrus-hide rope for corn. But pirates annexed everything, and hanged King Gudlaug at an unidentified spot named Straumeyarnes. His son Gylaug, on hearing the sad news, fitted out an expedition and hanged the pirates at Oddesund in the Limfjord, Jutland.

In later years the Earls of Haalogaland acquired property in Central Norway, either by marriage or conquest, and before the foundation of Norway in 872 had themselves moved south, though maintaining their overlordship of Haalogaland from a distance.

It is not, however, until the middle of the ninth century that any reference to events in North Norway can be considered to have an historical background.

The Account of Ottar of Troms (A.D. 875)

The earliest reliable account of North Norway was given verbally to King Alfred the Great of Wessex in about the year A.D. 875, and may be considered as the first 'Guidebook to the Land of the Midnight Sun.'

In A.D. 420 the Latin author *Orosius* had written a *History of Europe* as the Romans knew it in his days. More than four centuries later King Alfred himself translated it, and, since many northern European lands were known to him of which Orosius knew little or nothing, considerable additions were made to the original work. Amongst these is the story of *Ottar* the Haalo-galander, who, however, confined himself to geographical details and unfortunately no mention is made of Norway's history.

The 'plutocrat' Ottar probably left his home at the extreme north of Haalogaland (70°) in the month of May, and sailed down the Inner Lead to Skiringsal (near Tønsberg) and south to Hedeby (Slesvig), whence he would have hugged the coast of Frisia till he crossed the Channel. It was probably an ordinary trading voyage, when he would have bartered ermine and other furs, walrus tusks and ships-rope made of walrus-hide, eiderdown and other Arctic products, for iron implements, cloth, jewellery and even corn. The large vessels of his day carried thirty men, and these he would have had to maintain in England during a stay, which surely lasted till the following spring once again brought favourable weather for his return journey of more than 1,500 miles. It was an expensive voyage for Ottar, so the goods he brought and bought must have been of high value.

This is how Alfred wrote down Ottar's statement:

I live most northerly of all Norwegians in the north part of the country by the Western Sea. But land stretches still farther north and that is all waste land. There is pasture at only a few places and there the Finns (Lapps) are occasionally found. They hunt in winter and fish in the sea during summer. I wanted to know how far the land stretched to the north and whether people lived north of the waste land. So I sailed northwards along the coast for three days, and the whale-catchers never go farther than this. I had waste land to starboard and open sea to port all the time. Then I sailed northwards yet a further three days, when the land curved eastwards or there was a bay, I am not sure which it was (North Cape). There I had to wait for a more westerly or north-westerly wind, and then I sailed eastwards along the coast as far as I could sail in four days. There I had to wait for a due north wind, as the land curved southwards or a bay ran in, I do not know for certain which it was (Gandvika, White Sea). Then I sailed due south along the coast as far as I could come in five days. Here a large river ran inland (Varsuga) and we went up it. But the country on this side of the river (Bjarmeland) was thickly populated and we did not dare to go there for fear of trouble.

The country of the Finns (Lapps) was waste, and we had not come upon populated districts since we left home, except for a few fishermen, hunters and bird-catchers. The Bjarmer told us a lot about their country. Their language closely resembled that of the Finns (Lapps).

I undertook this journey to examine the country and to obtain walrus. The walrus has in its teeth a large fine bone and the hide is excellent for ships-rope. This whale is smaller than other whales as he is only 7 alen long. But at home in my own country there are whales which are 48 alen (? feet), and the largest is 50 alen long. I myself have killed 60 of these in two days.

When we returned home I owned 600 tame reindeer, of which 6 were decoys which the Finns (Lapps) put a high value on, as they tame the wild reindeer with them. I am one of the leading men in the country, but nevertheless I own no more than 20 cows, 20 sheep and 20 pigs. I use horses for the little ploughing I do.

But the most prized possession are the taxes the Finns (Lapps) pay, each according to his estate. . . .

In conclusion Ottar says that the province he dwelt in was called Haalogaland, and that no Norwegians lived to the north of him. Perhaps he meant by this that he was the most northerly 'plutocrat,' and it seems probable that he had his dwelling-house on Skjervøy (70°) or Karlsøy. He would also have possessed land at Lyngseidet (where he could have grown the little corn he required), and Alteidet (where he could have controlled his six hundred reindeer when they crossed that isthmus going north in June and south in September). Some of the bird-islands would have provided him with eiderdown, whilst the tax on the Lapps brought him skins of bear, marten, otter and of course ermine which was in such great demand in the Courts of Europe.

His statement that he ploughed with horses was no doubt caused by his surprise at the use of oxen for this purpose in England. It is probable that the little corn he grew was mainly used for production of maltings and spirit, and that importation of corn to North Norway was then as now a vital necessity.

It is on this priceless statement of Ottar in about 875 that the sagas can be weighed, since, for all the kernels of truth they may contain, they are historical novels rather than works of history.

Haalogaland under Harald Fairhair (872–933)

'Landnamabok' calls Grjotgard Herlaugsson 'Haaløygjajarl' and *not* Aamdarjarl, which seems to confirm that the earls exercised overlordship in Haalogaland beyond their earldom of Aamd. This *Earl Grjotgard* became master of the approaches to Trondheimfjord in about 850, and prepared the way for his son Haakon to rule at Lade (on the outskirts of Trondheim) as master of the ceremonies at the sacrificial altars there. The earls were thereafter known as 'Ladejarler.'

It was also in about 850 that *Harald Fairhair* was born, who, with the aid of Grjotgard's son Haakon, was to unify all the petty kingdoms and found the *Kingdom of Norway*. Harald would have been only fifteen years of age when he marched his forces over the Dovre (865) to find *Haakon Grjotgardsson* (*the elder*), a man of nearly fifty, overlord of the coast from

Tromsø to Molde, and holding more power in his hands than any other Norwegian has ever had.

The two mightiest men in Norway then agreed to unify the country, and the Earl accepted the young Harald as King of Haalogaland without a blow being struck. The friendship between these two great chiefs was cemented when Harald married Haakon's daughter Aasa, whilst two of Haakon's sons were killed fighting for Harald in the two battles of Solskjell (866 and 867).

Haakon Jarl Grjotgardsson (the elder) was himself killed in battle in about 868, leaving his magnificent heritage to his little grandson *Haakon Jarl Grjotgardsson (the younger)*, then an infant three years of age. His uncle Harald Fairhair became his guardian, and as such governed his Earldom (from Tromsø to Molde) until Haakon took it over on coming of age in about 883. And so for fifteen critical years in the unification of Norway the Province of Haalogaland came directly under the iron rule of the masterful Harald Fairhair.

Snorre states that Harald when he was fifty (A.D. 900) gave his sons royal prerogatives and divided the kingdom between them under his overlordship. It was *Erik Bloody Axe* who received Haalogaland, but since Haakon Jarl was then alive and in favour, Erik probably only received certain taxes and rents of places such as Sandnes which King Harald had arrogated to himself. *Haakon Jarl Grjotgardsson (the younger)* probably died about 920 and was succeeded as Ladejarl by his son *Sigurd.*

Distances were great to Haalogaland and there was always Folla to be crossed. So it is probable that the writ of neither king nor earl ran up there with any regularity, and the petty plutocrats would have lived and governed much as they pleased.

Torgar (now Torget, 65½°) was the seat of an ancient family, and in Egil's Saga we read that Bjaargolf was an old man before he took his second wife, and had already turned over control of Torgar to his son Brynjolf. His second wife, Hilderid, was acquired as the result of the old man having drawn her by lot as his dinner companion at a great feast he gave at Torgar. Bjaargolf became infatuated and sought out Hilderid at her

23

father's home on Leka island (65°), where he had become a 'new-rich' plutocrat. Bjaargolf threatened Hilderid's father with her rape if he did not consent to her marriage, which he did with a bad grace and for 27 grammes of gold—a very low price for a virgin. Hilderid bore him two sons, and directly the old man was dead Brynjolf packed all three back to Leka. But the sons had their revenge!

When Baard, the son of Brynjolf, died at the Battle of Hafrsfjord (872) he left his properties at Torgar and Sandnes, as also his widow Sigrid, to his great friend *Torolv Kveldulvsson*. The sons of Hilderid, being cheated of their rightful inheritance, proceeded to rouse the suspicions of Harald Fairhair that Torolv had great ambitions, and it all ended by the King surprising Torolv at Sandnes Castle and 'burning him in.' The mounds where this castle stood are prominent to this day, and at its foot lies the head of the narrow fjord where Torolv drew up his boats after their voyages to even faraway England. (It was at the time of Ottar.)

Torolv's nephew, *Egil*, in the celebrated 'Egils Saga,' described Torolv's journeys into 'Finnmark,' as all the wild hinterland was called in those days, to collect taxes from the Lapps in the form of furs. The King appointed some plutocrat his lieutenant, since 'finneferd' (Lapp journey) became a royal prerogative after the formation of the Kingdom of Norway, and was his main source of revenue. Torolv went across into what is now Sweden from his castle of Sandnessjøen, probably by way of Ranafjord and through the Umbukta of today. Egil gives a fascinating account of his journeyings.

The King then offered Sandnes and the twice-widowed Sigrid to Torolv's uncle, who accepted both. They moved a few miles south to fertile *Tjøtta*, where they founded a new plutocratic family that played a great part in Haalogaland history. Their son was Finn, who married Harald Fairhair's granddaughter, and their son, born on Tjøtta in about 920, was Øjvind Skaldespiller Finnsson—Norway's greatest skald.

There can be little doubt that Harald Fairhair's rule in Haalogaland, as guardian for the young Earl Haakon, was more harsh than the plutocrats there were accustomed from the Haaløygjajarler. Harald may have feared a rising, and so eliminated Torolv. During 'landnamstida' on Iceland around the year 900 the names are known of fifty-one men and women who migrated there from Nordland's coast owing to the grim rule of Haakon Jarl Grjotgardsson (the younger), but not a few of these would have left whilst Harald Fairhair was his guardian. Among these emigrants was a Haalogaland lady named 'Geirrid,' who built her new home in the middle of the highway, where stood a table loaded with food and drink. This woman is held up as a shining example of Haalogaland hospitality.

The reign of Harald Fairhair was the flowering period of the Vikings. Many of these set out from Haalogaland, not only on 'The Western Way' and 'Eastern Way,' but also on 'The Northern Way' to the lands of the fur-bearing animals. They returned as mighty sea-kings to their plutocratic centres (or founded new ones), bringing back rich booty and a number of slaves, several of these from Ireland. But the concept of slavery does not fit in with northern ideas, and they seem to have been quickly absorbed into the community.

Harald Fairhair took a serving-wench to bed when he was seventy years old, and produced a boy who was later to be blessed in Norway by the name of *Haakon the Good*. The birth took place on board one of Sigurd Jarl's ships, and the Earl 'threw water over him'—a heathen baptismal rite.

Erik Bloody-Axe

So little is known about Erik Bloody-Axe's activities in Haalogaland and his relations with Haakon Jarl Grjotgardsson (the younger)—indeed the whole existence of the latter is enveloped in mystery. Erik went on many a viking voyage and at least once to Bjarmeland. For on the return journey his men landed in modern Finnmark, to find the most beautiful of maidens in distress. Her story was that her father sent her up from Haalogaland to learn magic from two Lapp trolls. She learnt a lot, but then both trolls insisted on marrying her despite her remonstrances. Erik's men killed the trolls and took *Gunhild* on board, and thus she became the mother of Erik's sons.

The Saga is obviously romance, but its author probably wished to attribute the evils that fell upon the land to the hated Queen Gunhild, and to the supernatural powers she had acquired from the gentle and harmless Lapps. Two years later the aged Harald died; Erik Bloody-Axe fled to the Orkneys (935) with his troll-queen, and later became Lord of Northumberland.

The Reign of Haakon the Good (935–961)

Haakon, son of Harald and his serving-wench, was sent to the Court of Athelstan of England when a child. It was surely *Sigurd Ladejarl* who recalled the fifteen-year-old boy, and became his right-hand in the conquest of Norway and expulsion of Erik Bloody-Axe. Sigurd—who was 'the wisest man in Norway'— gave Haakon a great reception at Lade and they joined forces. The agreement gave Sigurd Jarl sovereign authority over North and Central Norway, though presumably with the reservation of 'finneferd' and Lapp taxes for the royal coffers. But the Earl had to provide military forces to combat the sons of Gunhild, Haalogaland being assessed at fourteen armed vessels. There was complete understanding between earl and king, and when a son was born to the former—on the first night of 'Yule' 937—it was Haakon that 'threw water over him' and gave the boy his own name. This baby became the mighty heathen chieftain Haakon Jarl.

We hear nothing about Haalogaland during this reign, since both earl and king had enough trouble in Southern Norway. So it can be assumed that the plutocrats and viking 'sea-kings' had their own way up there.

Haakon the Good was killed in battle in 961, and two years later the great Earl Sigurd was 'burnt-in' not far from Lade.

Haakon Ladejarl (963–995)

After the murder of Sigurd Jarl his son took up the fight against the 'sons of Gunhild.' Haakon fled to Denmark and excited that country's interest in acquiring the sovereignty of Norway. Crop failures and bad weather conditions through a series of years were blamed on Gunhild's 'trolldom' and that of her spawn, and so Haakon gained sufficient support from the masses to win the celebrated Battle of Hjørungavaag (985) near Stadt against the Jomsvikings, whom the King of Denmark had sent to Norway on his errands.

Haakon Jarl ruled Norway as the last of the heathens. His miserable end came in 995. None of the sons of Gunhild exercised any form of sovereignty over Haalogaland, which lay outside the battle area and was left to itself and its plutocrats. But from 876 till the death of Haakon Ladejarl it was the earls who possessed full sovereign powers within their patriarchal territory.

Culture and Verse in Heathen Haalogaland

North Norwegian poetry reflects life in the far north—we sense the long summer days and can hear the call of swans that build their nests on the banks of the placid lakes. The long winter nights can be felt, and we see the hunter putting on his skis to search for the tracks of brown bears. The shoals of herring setting into land become alive in our imagination, whilst the Midnight Sun prompts visions of fabled islands and rocks on the far horizon.

The *Elder Edda* was in part created in Haalogaland, likewise the *Song of Valund*, *Grimnismaal* and perhaps *Skirnesmaal*. And here lived *Øjvind Skaldespiller*. His poems are rich in everyday happenings which acquire colour and movement in their magnificent natural surroundings. There are pictures of tasty herrings in long nets, of duck in flight, and of snow still lying at Midsummer so that goats have to be fed in the byres on birch-leaves.

The North Norwegian School of Poetry was also influenced by voyages to the shores of Britain, both in subject-matter and in loan-words, which we meet for the first time in the *Song of Valund the Smith* and in *Thor's Journey to Hymer*. None of the ancient skalds ranked higher than Øjvind Skaldespiller. *Grimnismaal* was composed about 950. Its kernel is an old North Norwegian folk-saga. *The Cormorants on Farther Røst* is a later version of the same saga. But the background for them all was the ancient North Norwegian (and Irish) belief in the Fairyland that lay hidden out in the ocean. Utrøst and Utvega were such lands, whilst And y, Svinøy in Brønnøy, Vega and Sølen beyond Vega had once been fairylands but had materialized.

Around the year 900 tales of sea-voyages to 'Fairyland' were common in Haalogaland. The author of *Grimnismaal* knew all about them. Some authorities believe that Øjvind Skaldespiller wrote *Grimnismaal*, there is no certainty.

The *Song of Valund* is about the old smith Valund, who together with his brothers meets the swan-maidens from the south, wins one of them and loses her again. He is later captured by King Nidad, who has him hamstrung and lands him on a lonely rock. There he shall forge articles of beauty for the king. But Valund takes complete revenge. He kills the king's sons, rapes his daughters, and then flies away on wings of his own making. This song was composed about 900 by a Haalogalending who had visited northern England and there heard a similar song about an ingenious smith. The poem has the atmosphere of the far north, and we learn that the Samer (Lapps) use skis and trap wolves and other wild animals. We read of the 'singing-swans' that come flying from the south and build nests by the large placid lakes far beyond human dwellings. In the verse we sense the long winter nights.

In the *Edda* Valund and his brothers are made out to be Lapps who use skis, and hammer gold out of the mountains. They dwell in 'wolf-valleys' and come to the wolf-lake where they meet the maidens who come flying from the south in the plumage of swans and lie down on the shores of the lake. In no other Edda-song is the life of humans in relation to nature more vividly described. Therefore Valund the Smith lived long in folk-memory, and the verses about him travelled from Haalogaland by the trade routes till they reached Gotland. There, on a stone a thousand years old, we can see today a picture of Valund and his smithy, with the severed heads of the sons of Nidad. And there is Valund himself on his skis, and the maidens in their swan-plumage.

Øjvind Skaldespiller was the last great Norwegian skald, and was so nicknamed because he towered above all other skalds. He was born on the island of Tjøtta (65¾°) in Helgeland in about 920, his mother being a granddaughter of Harald Fairhair. He is first mentioned in the sagas prior to the Battle of Fitjar (961), in which he took part. He thereupon composed *Haakonarmaal* in honour of King Haakon the Good, which is without question one of the finest lays in Old Norse verse. Øjvind was present at the Battle of Hjørungavaag (985) as lieutenant to Haakon Jarl, but he was then an old man. Thereafter he wrote *Haaløygjatal* in honour of Earl Haakon and all his family. He probably died about 990, and with the death of those two old heathens a new chapter opens in the history of North Norway.

The Reign of Olav Trygvesson (995-1000)

The life of Olav Trygvesson, a grandson of Harald Fairhair, was one of conflict from cradle to grave. He had ravaged England in company with Svend Forkbeard, and became one of the most renowned Viking chieftains. Having been converted to Christianity on one of these expeditions he was baptized in the Scilly Isles.

After this be abandoned piracy and, in 995, sailed for Trondheim on hearing that the masses had risen against Haakon Ladejarl. Olav caused that mighty old heathen's head to be set up on Trondheim's island of Munkholmen for the populace to stone, and he smashed up the idols and sacrificial altars at Lade nearby. Haakon Jarl's two sons, Erik and Svend, had to save their lives by hasty flight.

In 996 Olav Trygvesson sailed north with the intention of implanting Christianity on Haalogaland, but before he had crossed Folla he learnt that a strong force from the north was on its way to challenge his further progress, and so Olav returned to Trondheimsfjord. It seems safe to infer from these proceedings that the Haalogaland plutocrats considered themselves entirely independent after the fall of Haakon Jarl in 995, and banded themselves together to assert this independence. Their action was

29

not so much against Christianity as opposed to any form of southern overlordship. Three of these leaders are mentioned as captains of the defending force, viz.: Tore Hjort from Vaagan (Kabelvaag, $68\frac{1}{4}°$) in Lofoten, Haarek from Tjøtta ($65\frac{3}{4}°$), and Øjvind Kinnriva, who seems to have been Haarek's nearest neighbour.

Haarek had become the most powerful of Haalogaland chieftains, though his father—old Øjvind Skaldespiller—had left but few worldly goods. But Haarek when young had gone on viking and trading voyages, amassing considerable wealth with which he bought up all the small landowners on Tjøtta, and built himself a fine hall there. The sagas relate that in 998 Haarek was enticed down to Trondheim where he accepted baptism, perhaps in return for a grant of full sovereignty over not merely his own district but also that of Øjvind Kinnriva. The latter is said to have been inveigled by Haarek down to Trondheim, where he refused baptism and was tortured to death.

King Olav sailed north in 999 to christen Haalogaland, at least so it is stated in the sagas. He reached Tjøtta early in the year where he was well received by Haarek, whom he made his 'lieutenant' in Helgeland and gave authority for 'finneferd' and to collect tribute from the Lapps. These privileges would have been the same that Torolv Kveldulvsson lost to Harald Fairhair in 877, and extended over the 'forest-lapps' who roamed the hinterland beyond Umbukta (66°) in what is now Sweden.

The Plutocrats to the north of Haarek, however, rose against King Olav. Tore Hjort manned a large ship in Lofoten, and was joined by the great chief of Saltenfjord named 'Raud den ramme.' The latter was a great sacrificer to the gods, and well versed in the magic of the trolls. He owned the finest ship in the north, that had no doubt been built at Rognan (67°), at the head of Saltenfjord, where many splendid vessels yet take the water. The royal fleet met the men of Salten and Lofoten off Ranafjord, where Tore Hjort and Raud got the worst of it and fled. Raud rowed out to sea and, being a troll, managed to raise a fair wind that took his fine ship home to Salten. But Tore Hjort beached

30

his boat and took to the hills, to be overtaken by Olav's hound 'Vige,' and then killed by the King himself.

Olav then sailed north to settle with Raud, but the 'maelstrøm' at the entrance of Saltenfjord was violent for a whole week— even as is often the case today. So with a fair wind the King made for Andøya and christened the populous district of Aamd. Returning to Saltenfjord the maelstrøm remained disturbed for several days, until Bishop Sigurd said several prayers in the bows of Olav's vessel, when the whirlpools calmed in mid-stream and the King sailed through a placid channel between two series of mountainous waves that were beating on both shores. They found Raud asleep, but when Olav invited him to adopt Christianity he refused. So an adder was put in his mouth, which refused to proceed farther when Raud blew on it. A 'lur' was then placed in his throat, the adder in the lur and a red-hot iron on the adder's tail. It passed through his alimentary tract till it reached his stomach, when it bit a way out through his side. Thus died Raud den ramme at Godøy in Saltenfjord.

The magnificent vessel with its dragon head on the prow was named 'Ormen' (the serpent) by Olav, who sailed it down to Trondheim, where it was used as a model for war-boats over a long period. Thus did the long-dead naval architects of Rognan earn a measure of immortality.

Eminent authorities cast doubts on the above fantastic stories from the sagas. Some Norwegian historians do not believe that Olav Trygvesson made any attempt to Christianize Haalogaland, or to affirm his sovereignty there, other than that which he abandoned in 996. It may be that he succeeded in eliminating Tore Hjort and Raud on their trading journeys to Southern Norway, but the probability is that the plutocrats retained their sovereign independence throughout the whole of Olav Trygvesson's short reign. Indeed he had enough trouble to cope with elsewhere and, since neither Haarek himself nor a single vessel from Haalogaland took part in the Battle of Svolder, it seems likely that that province did not obey Olav's mobilization orders, for the simple reason that he exercised no authority there.

Olav Trygvesson jumped overboard after defeat at the Battle

of Svolder off the island of Rügen (in the Baltic) in the year 1000, and it was Erik Jarl, the son of Haakon Ladejarl, who was the final instrument in his death and thus avenged his father.

Haalogaland under Erik Jarl and Einar Tambarskjelver (1000–1016)

The fall of Olav Trygvesson was a disaster for Norway, which lost its unity and was split up amongst the victors of Svolder. The kings of Denmark and Sweden and the earls Erik and Svend staked their claims, but the foreign kings left much of their sovereign authority with the two earls who became the actual rulers of Norway. They had both accepted baptism but made little effort to enforce Christian rites, so presumably much of Haalogaland, under the overlordship of Erik Jarl, continued to propitiate its gods with sacrifices during these two decades.

Erik Jarl had full sovereignty over the ancient territories of the Haaløygjajarler, so that relations between earl and plutocrats would have been by ancient custom. But in 1015 Erik took an army to England at the request of his brother-in-law Canute the Great, who made him Earl of Northumberland in 1017. He passed over his sovereign rights in Norway to his seventeen-year-old son Haakon, whose regent and adviser was the famous Einar Tambarskjelver (so nicknamed because of his enormous quivering paunch). The latter, although he had fought by the side of Olav Trygvesson at Svolder, made his peace with Earl Erik and married his sister Bergliot. Soon after Earl Erik had left for England the young Haakon was captured by Olav, the new claimant for Norway's throne and later to be known as 'St. Olav.' Young Haakon's life was spared by his taking an oath never to fight against Olav, and he then sailed for England to join Canute the Great. This left Einar Tambarskjelver as sole ruler of Haalogaland and, in league with Earl Svend, he repelled the first attacks which Olav made against the Earl's territories.

Following the year 1000 there were two plutocrats in Haalogaland who towered above all others, viz.: Tore Hund of Bjarkøy (69°) and Haarek of Tjøtta (66°). The former seems to have had control over what is now Troms Fylke and Lofoten, whilst Haarek lorded it over Helgeland and Salten. The pre-eminence of their positions supports the saga tales of the elimination by Olav Trygvesson of Tore Hjort of Lofoten, Raud den ramme of Salten, and of Øjvind Kinnriva of Helgeland.

Bjarkøy is a small island lying in the centre of the Bay of Senja, with the three large and populous islands of Hinnøy, Senja and Andøy surrounding it. The island itself with its fertile soil formed a splendid home for the prominent family which is first mentioned in connection with Tore Hund in about the year 1000. The name Bjarkøy is the same as 'Birka' near modern Stockholm, which up till that time was the most important trading centre in Scandinavia. We hear of a 'Karl of Bjarkøy' at the close of the ninth century, who may have been the ancestor of Tore Hund and thus the progenitor of one of Norway's finest families through several centuries.

The Reign of Olav the Saint (1016–1030)

On Palm Sunday, 1016, Olav the Saint defeated Earl Svend, Einar Tambarskjelver and Haarek of Tjøtta at the Battle of Nesjar, when all three succeeded in escaping.

But it was not until 1019 that Olav began to take an interest in Haalogaland, his method of subduing it being to enforce the adoption of Christianity. It was to Haarek that Olav turned when he decided to travel north. The king had spent the winter of 1019–1020 in Nidaros (Trondheim), and sent word to Haarek at Tjøtta that he proposed to visit Haalogaland next summer and would travel 'to the end of the country.' Haarek received him with much feasting, whereupon Olav made him his 'lieutenant' and granted him the revenues which he had enjoyed under the previous overlords. This meant that Haarek was deprived of the sovereignty he had possessed during the long interregnum, and that he was now less independent of the King than he had been of the earls.

Olav proceeded north and christened all Haalogaland, and the sagas relate that Tore Hund of Bjarkøy—the most powerful man in the north—was on this occasion also made 'king's lieutenant.' This meant that, like Haarek, his independence had been restricted. Snorre then says: 'The sons of the powerful peasants (plutocrats) joined the train of King Olav. High above these towered, each in his own half of Haalogaland, Haarek and Tore Hund, who were separated from each other by the high mountains north of the Vestfjord.'

Olav found it advisable to reduce the spheres of influence of the plutocrats, his method being to transfer sections of his 'lieutenancies' to low-born upstarts. He did not actively begin this policy until he sat firmly on the throne, but this of course aroused the enmity of all plutocrats. Haarek's turn came in 1024 when Olav granted the northern part of South Haalogaland (? Dønna) to Asmund Grankelson. Haarek disputed the possession of some bird-islands where eiderdown was collected in large quantities, and which Asmund claimed. In 1028 he took his revenge by 'burning-in' Asmund's father, and did so with impunity—an indication of the lawless conditions pertaining in Haalogaland, and that the King's writ did not run there.

Haarek of Tjøtta was the hero of a remarkable saga-tale in 1027, when his ship was accompanying the fleet of Olav into the Baltic. Canute lay in the Sound with so powerful a fleet that Olav decided to leave his ships at Kalmar and return to Norway overland. Haarek declined to accompany him, saying: 'I am old and heavy, and little accustomed to walking, so I could not return to Norway by land.' To which Olav replied: 'Come with us Haarek, we will carry you if you cannot walk.' But Haarek camouflaged his ship as a trader, and thus slipped through Canute's mighty fleet—though it has been suggested that Haarek was even then on the best of terms with Canute and secretly at loggerheads with Olav. Haarek sailed north direct to Tjøtta, where he continued to exercise sovereign authority over the whole of southern Haalogaland. There he remained till the year of his murder at Trondheim in 1039 at the age of eighty.

Tore Hund of Bjarkøy

The murder of Tore Hund's relative Asbjørn Selsbane in 1024, at the instigation of the King, put an end to any friendship that might have existed between Olav and his lieutenant in northern Haalogaland. So he had little consideration for two of Olav's 'hirdmen' (bodyguard)—Karle and Gunnstein—who were his near neighbours from the island of Langøy in Vesteraalen. They went in company, however, on a trading voyage to the White Sea in 1026, and on the return journey Tore speared Karle at Gjesvaer (close to the North Cape), whilst Gunnstein escaped with his vessel hotly pursued by Tore. At Lenvik (69¼°) Gunnstein, overhauled by Tore, ran his ship ashore and was received and hidden by a troll-woman, whilst Tore Hund annexed the cargo and sailed home to Bjarkøy. In the autumn Gunnstein communicated the news of the murder of his brother (Olav's hirdman) to the King, and in the spring of 1027 Tore was called to account for his nefarious deed. At Vaagan (Kabelvaag) he was heavily fined at the 'ting' by the King's plenipotentiary. After a few paltry sums had been paid over, Tore Hund slipped out of the harbour and sailed direct to England to King Canute.

Sigurd of Trondenes

Tore Hund had a brother, Sigurd, who lived at Trondenes on the north-east corner of Hinnøy. He was not a king's lieutenant, and so never a national figure, but in his own district was a great leader and, in heathen times, held three sacrificial feasts annually —on October 14th, January 14th and a third in the summer. When he accepted baptism he continued these feasts—after the harvest, at Christmas and at Easter. Trondenes was a busy centre during those feasts, which his son Asbjørn continued after his father's death. But for a succession of years the grain crop failed throughout Norway. So Asbjørn went south to collect corn for the feasts, only to learn that King Olav had prohibited movement of corn reserves from the south. His powerful relations down there, however, procured what he required by evading the King's order through a legal quibble. Then one of Olav's 'low-born upstarts' seized the corn, and the proud young Haalogalander Asbjørn contrived to murder the King's agent in Olav's presence at Eastertide. The saga gives a lively description of the severed head falling at the King's feet, etc. But the story gives an early example of the demand for corn in Northern Norway—a demand that must be satisfied from more temperate climes till this very day.

Canute the Great—Svend—Alfifa (1028–35)

In 1028 King Canute left Denmark for Trondheim with Tore Hund in company, and King Olav had to flee the country. Canute was acclaimed 'King of Norway,' and then appointed Tore Hund his Lieutenant for northern Haalogaland and Haarek of Tjøtta in southern. They were granted 'finneferd' in their respective areas, and other considerable perquisites.

Tore Hund seems to have learnt of the intention of Olav the Saint to return to Norway to reclaim his kingdom from Canute. It was on his return from 'finneferd' in 1030 that Tore decreed mobilization throughout north Haalogaland to raise a force to resist Olav. Tore sailed south as soon as he was ready.

The epoch-making Battle of *Stiklestad* (some fifty miles north of Trondheim) was fought on July 28–29, 1030, when the leaders of the peasant forces were Tore Hund, Haarek of Tjøtta and Kalv Arnesøn. A Haalogalander named 'Torstein the boat-builder' was the first to wound the 'Saint of Norway' with a blow from an axe above the knee, and then Tore Hund stuck his famous spear into Olav's stomach below the cuirass, whilst at the same moment a third wound was inflicted on his throat. Olav the Saint died of these three wounds on July 29, 1030, and Tore Hund laid the body out on the field and covered it with a cloth. He stated later that when he dried the blood from the King's mouth the most amazing miracles occurred, and he was so impressed with the saintliness of the dead Olav that he was the first person of consequence to believe in his sanctity. An eclipse of the sun darkened the world of the homegoing Haalogalanders, and that awe-inspiring phenomenon also contributed to the elevation of Olav.

Tore Hund himself never had a peaceful moment after hearing the prayers of the dying king when he thrust the spear into his body. That powerful Haalogaland chieftain went to London, where he so impressed Canute with Olav's miracles that that king promised large sums to the shrine of Olav. Tore Hund went to Jerusalem to find peace of soul—but never returned.

With the foundation of the empire of Canute the Great the Viking Age came to an end and piracy virtually ceased. Henceforth voyages were for the purpose of legitimate trade. And, after the death of his adversary Olav, it seemed that Canute's great 'Empire of the North Sea' would survive for all time. His son Svend was acclaimed 'King of Norway,' and Canute sent Svend's mother Alfifa (who was his own first wife) to act as regent, supported by several Danish advisers. They promulgated many new laws which were not appreciated by their Norwegian subjects, whose belief in the sanctity of their dead King Olav was sedulously fanned by such leaders as old Einar Tambarskjelver. Unrest was created, and so Norway seceded from Canute's empire a few months before his death. This was the first of his dominions to break away.

It is probable that Sigurd took over control of Haalogaland north of the Vestfjord when his father Tore Hund vanished to the Holy Land in a fit of remorse, whilst old Haarek of Tjøtta continued his control between Folla and the Vestfjord. Danish sovereignty in Haalogaland would have been purely nominal in these years.

The Reign of Magnus the Good (1035–47)

This young son of Olav the Saint was brought back from Russia by two of his father's opponents, who took the precaution to extract an assurance of amnesty for all that had taken the other side. This promise was not kept, and one of those to suffer was old Haarek of Tjøtta. The old man seems to have had doubts as to the value of Magnus' promise since he waited four years to pay homage, and it does not appear that Magnus attempted to cross Folla to extract it. When Haarek presented himself at Magnus' Court in Trondheim he was set upon by his old enemy Asmund Grankelson, whose axe was too flimsy to finish him off.

So King Magnus lent his own heavier axe, which clove the brain of the eighty-year-old Tjøtta chief—in the year 1039.

The Reign of King Harald Hardraade (1047–66)

Magnus the Good agreed shortly before his death to share his throne with his uncle Harald Hardraade, the last of the Viking kings, who had amassed great wealth from his operations around Miklagaard (Constantinople) and in Russia.

It is known that in about 1050 Harald made a voyage to the Arctic. It may be that he travelled along the coast of Haalogaland, but there are divided opinions as to his route. East Greenland, Spitsbergen and Bjarmeland have all been favourites with eminent authorities. Adam of Bremen wrote that the King wished to discover 'how large the northern ocean was,' but it is more probable that the procuring of furs was the main objective, and so Finnmark and Murmansk were the most likely route.

In Haalogaland the son of Haarek, Einar Fluga, arrogated to himself a very special position. He was made 'sysselman' by Harald, and granted 'finneferd' as the King's agent. Now no one was allowed to trade or even journey into the hinterland of the Lapps without special permission from the King or his sysselman, and both kept a sharp lookout that this decree was obeyed. Anybody found with furs who had not such permission was in a perilous situation. Einar Fluga lived on Tjøtta as his father before him.

In the autumn of 1066 King Harald sailed with a mighty fleet of 240 larger vessels to conquer England, where he was defeated and killed at the Battle of Stamfordbridge, near York. And so Harald Hardraade, who founded the city of Oslo, did not create a Norwegian kingdom in England, but it is fascinating to speculate upon what the history of England would have been if a Norwegian had ruled there and had repelled William the Norman who, so it happened, landed at Hastings a short while after Harald's death.

The year 1066 was a fateful one in Norwegian as in English history. In that year whatever imperialistic ambitions may have been nursed in Norway were smothered for all time, whilst England saw the birth of such!

Means of Livelihood in Ancient Haalogaland

It was the ocean that provided the inhabitants of Haalogaland with their means of subsistence. Away from the coasts of the fjords and sea the only human beings were the nomad Lapps with their reindeer herds.

The *Seal* was perhaps the most valuable of all animals, since it provided warmth, light and clothing. The earliest laws decreed 'close-seasons' for their preservation.

Whale also played an important part in economy, as the story of Ottar tells us. Walrus hide provided ships-rope for export as well as for the needs of Haalogaland fishermen.

Cod and *Herring* fisheries were a constant source of food for the local inhabitants. Indeed 'torsk'—the modern Norwegian word for cod—is the old Norse name for 'dried fish.' The drying of cod into 'stokkfish' for export goes back to the earliest days. Torolv Kveldulvsson operated herring fishery in 872, and when the herring shoals deserted the coast in the middle of the tenth century it was regarded as a national disaster.

Eiderdown was collected from the 'bird islands,' and is mentioned by Ottar as one of the taxes levied on the Lapps. The eggs of sea-birds were also a valuable article of food at certain seasons.

Cultivation of Soil produced a small amount of corn and cattle. Ploughs, sickles and scythes have been found in graves. Barley ripened early in the long daylight, and Torolv Kveldulvsson owned a 'large corn-barn' where 800 men sat down at table.

Furs were the most important export article from Haalogaland. Torolv Kveldulvsson, Haarek of Tjøtta and Tore Hund carried these direct to England, and Ottar did likewise via Skiringsal and Hedeby. We read of the Bjarmeland voyages in search of furs through nearly four hundred years, with Haalogalanders as their leaders.

Corn was imported from Southern Norway and Denmark,

39

whilst other imports were fine clothing, ornaments and wine for the plutocrats, and honey for making mead.

Boat-building. The only fairly well preserved boat from North Norway is the 'Baardset' boat. It was dug out of a swamp on North Kvaløy (70°), has been reconstructed, and gives the earliest information on ship construction in the north. It was clinker-built and of pine, about 40 feet long and 8 feet beam, with eight or nine pairs of oars. Its date is probably around A.D. 700, and it was built by Norwegians—not by Lapps, who are also known to have put boats together at that period. This Baardset boat would be three hundred years older than the famous 'Ormen,' which Olav Trygvasson is said to have seized at Godøy in Saltenfjord in about 998. Both these ancient vessels may well have been constructed at Rognan in Saltdal, which has for centuries been the shipyard of North Norway. 'Torstein the boatbuilder' from Haalogaland, who gave St. Olav his first wound, may well have come from Rognan!

PART II

FROM OLAV KYRRE (1066) TO END OF DYNASTIC INDEPENDENCE (1319)

Haalogaland under Olav the Peaceful (1066–93)

WHEN King Olav Kyrre returned home after his father's defeat by King Harold of England he brought several English refugees with him. Among these was Ketil Krok, who was a son of Earl Tosti and thus a nephew of King Harold Godwinson. King Olav is said to have found a rich wife for Ketil in Haalogaland and made him his 'Lieutenant' there. It seems probable that he was the progenitor of the Torgar (Torghatten) family who carried the English name of William (Viljam) through many centuries and controlled a large district from that island of Torghatten.

The scanty ruins of a church dedicated to St. Knud of Denmark (died 1086) were discovered at Tilrem on Brønnøy in 1934. It would be strange to find such a dedication so far away from Denmark were it not that Olav Kyrre's queen was St. Knud's sister. Perhaps, however, Ketil Krok built it, for St. Knud was his cousin.

One of the few stone churches in ancient Haalogaland is at Gildeskaal (67°), a name which perhaps dates from Olav Kyrre since he encouraged the formation of 'guilds' after the English model, to promote social security and sickness benefits.

Magnus Barefoot (1093–1103)

For a while Norway had two acclaimed kings at one time, since Magnus' accession was disputed by two powerful chieftains in the south. In 1095 a rebellion was started by Tore of Steig (Gudbrandsdal) whom Magnus attacked near Trondheim. Tore

41

fled north overland, to take to the sea again and commence pillage in Haalogaland. The bandits ravaged all the way to Bjarkøy, whence Tore Hund's grandson Vidkunn Jonson had to flee for his life. Tore the rebel seized all movables and set fire to the dwellings, of which the skald sang:—

> In Bjarkøy's centre
> The Hall burns
> The most magnificent I wot of.

Vidkunn and his father made all haste to King Magnus who was on his way north, where the rebels did not expect him. They had turned south and continued their plundering till they reached Harm in Brønnøy, when, on sighting the King's ships, they endeavoured to escape. Tore and Egil went ashore at Hestun on Hamnøy in the belief it was the mainland, and there the King's ship overhauled them. They were hanged on the island of Vomma, Tore being so heavy that when his body dropped his neck broke in two, leaving the head hanging solo.

In 1098 King Magnus Barefoot made his first voyage to Ireland. Vidkunn Jonson of Bjarkøy, as also Sigurd and Ulv Raneson of Steigen (68°) accompanied him. These three Haalogalanders were also with him on his second and final voyage westwards in 1101–3. In a fight on an Ulster beach in 1103 Magnus fell, along with Ulv Raneson of Steigen. Vidkunn Jonson was with the King at the last, when Magnus implored him to save himself by flight. Before doing so he killed the man who slew his king and was the last to leave the scene of battle, with Sigurd Raneson just ahead of him.

The sons of Magnus never forgot Vidkunn's heroism, and he remained their Lieutenant in Haalogaland till he was a very old man. Sigurd the Crusader sent his own son Magnus (the Blind) up to Bjarkøy to be brought up by Vidkunn Jonson.

Øiestein, Sigurd the Crusader and Olav (1103–30)

The 'Divine Right of Kings' was accepted as an axiom in ancient Norway, all the king's sons having equal rights of succession. Since many of these old kings were lusty fellows who cast their fancies over several women, a multiplicity of offspring—legitimate and illegitimate—brought great inconvenience and distress to the realm of Norway.

But the three sons of Magnus Barefoot (so-called because he wore the Scottish kilt) caused no trouble in the land, since they shared the throne in fraternal peace and each exercised authority in the particular sphere of kingship that appealed to him.

Øiestein (Augustine) was the ideal administrator, who introduced reforms in North Norwegian life. His memory is kept green in Kabelvaag (Lofoten) by the massive statue gazing across the Vestfjord. In a suit of law in 1115 we have the first definite evidence that Lofoten fish was a major article of export, and it was in Øiestein's time that Vaagan (Kabelvaag) grew into a small town as the place of assembly for the fishermen of Haalogaland. Here and at Trondenes he built churches, and endowed them with lands. He caused barracks to be erected at Vaagan to house the fishermen during the cod season. 'Vaagan Silver'—small coins used at the fisheries there—circulated over all Norway under that name.

Around 1100 there was considerable prosperity in the North, as can be seen from the 'Frostating Law' (the legal code valid in Haalogaland at that period), which mentioned such articles as velvet, finely woven bed-curtains, eiderdown quilts, silver vessels, gold ornaments and precious stones. Also it was customary at large houses to keep valuable pet dogs.

Shipping also flourished in Haalogaland. The ancient trade routes still went westwards, forty ships sailed every summer to Iceland and others to the Shetlands and East Anglia. There were also voyages to Greenland and along the coast of Finnmark to Bjarmeland and the White Sea.

Taxes were reduced, and customs and shipping levies abolished. Merchants and travellers could go where they wished in Norway. The peasants in Haalogaland were given back their 'common' land, but the King retained monopoly of purchase of all furs north of Vennesund (65°)—the ancient boundary between Trøndelag and Helgeland.

King Sigurd the Crusader left Norway in the autumn of 1107 on his fantastic crusade to the Holy Land which gave to the world one of the most thrilling epics of the sea. This has been immortalized in Edvard Grieg's famous opera *Sigurd Jorsalafarer*, and there was surely many a Haalogalander on that eventful voyage though no names have come down to us.

After King Sigurd's return the famous legal proceedings commenced in 1113 between him and Sigurd Raneson of Steigen (68°), that grand old warrior who had remained to the last with King Magnus Barefoot on the Ulster beach in 1103. King Magnus had granted 'finneferd' to him for the duration of his own reign and those of his sons. Sigurd Raneson had married King Magnus' half-sister Skjaldvor, his own sister being Sigrid, 'a very beautiful woman,' who was raped after a festive evening by King Sigurd Jorsalafarer and forcibly (?) attached to him as his mistress. Sigurd Raneson accused the King of bringing shame on his family, whilst the King retaliated by calling him a thief in his administration of 'finneferd.'

In the following year (1114) King Sigurd put forward his claim for deficiency payments on 'finneferd' against Sigurd Raneson at the City Court in Trondheim. Sigurd Raneson declared that because he had saved the life of King Magnus Barefoot in Sweden, the latter had given him his half-sister to wife and also 'finneferd' and the right to trade with the Lapps for so long as King Magnus and his sons lived, against the payment of 60 marks to the Crown annually. King Sigurd maintained that his father had no right to depute 'finneferd' for a longer period than that of his own life. King Øiestein intervened that this case could not be argued at a City Court since it came under a higher law than those dealt with there.

Those who had their domicile in Steigen held their ordinary 'ting' on Kjefsøy, a tiny island with good landing facilities lying just south of Store Molla in the Vestfjord. The Kjefsøy-ting had the whole of the northern part of Haalogaland as its area, the boundary to the southern half being Brennsund near Kjerringøy.

King Sigurd summoned Sigurd Raneson to this 'ting,' where the case was refused when King Øiestein explained that since Sigurd Raneson was the King's Lieutenant he must appear before the 'ting' of the whole province, namely Trondenes-ting. So King Sigurd summoned him there, whereupon King Øiestein affirmed that the case was now one between two kings and therefore was a matter for the 'law-ting'—the Frostating. King Sigurd then brought the case to the Frostating in 1115, which was that year held at Trondheim, the legal luminary Jon Mørnev being its president.

The pundits gave the ruling that a Norwegian king could grant privileges for indefinite periods, but that to be legal such privileges must be proclaimed at all the three 'law-tings,' i.e. Frostating, Gulating, and Eisivating. Sigurd Raneson could not produce evidence that he had so proclaimed his privileges for longer than King Magnus' lifetime, and therefore it would appear he had lost his case. But the saga-writer thought otherwise, since he states that King Sigurd wanted it laid down by the 'law-ting' that no king of Norway could in the future grant privileges for longer than his own lifetime.

As King Øiestein and King Olav wished otherwise it was agreed to draw lots—one to each of the three kings—and King Sigurd won. King Øiesten then objected that it was unfair to make the new law retrospective, though according to the former practice it would seem that Sigurd Raneson had no rights to 'finneferd' after King Magnus' death, as he could not produce evidence of the necessary proclamations at the three 'tings.' King Øiestein, however, maintained that the case had been refused, firstly at the City Court, then at Kjefsøy, and finally at Trondenes, and when three 'tings' had refused a case it could not be brought up again. The saga-writer says this was confirmed by Jon Mørnev, though there is no such provision in the Frostating Code as it has come down to us. And so the case was refused, and King Sigurd left the 'ting' declaring that there was yet another way of getting judgment which he understood as well as did his brother.

King Sigurd had decided to commence fighting the next day,

but late in the evening Sigurd Raneson surrendered himself to that king to prevent the bloodshed a fraticidal quarrel would engender. King Sigurd made it a condition that he should pronounce judgment, which was that Sigurd Raneson pay 5 marks in gold to each of the three kings that very next day. The latter managed to raise exactly 5 marks, which first Øiestein and then Olav refused. When King Sigurd learnt of his brothers' actions he would not lag behind in magnanimity and handed back the 5 marks to Sigurd Raneson. Whereupon, says the saga-writer, the two Sigurds became firm friends and lived together happily ever after.

It is difficult to deduce how much of this famous legal dispute is genuine history, or to what extent the Icelandic saga-writer let his fancy take charge. Probably a large part of it is fiction, since it seems improbable that both kings with their armed forces would have been willing to remain for months at a stretch in the north of Haalogaland over a paltry matter of 15 gold marks.

Sigurd Raneson of Steigen remained in possession of 'finne-ferd,' and his son Nicholas Skjaldvorsen also retained it until he was killed by the rebel 'birch-legs' in 1176.

The Great Civil War—first phase (1131–79)

A tragic century opened for Norway on the death of Sigurd Jorsalafarer. Claims to kingship were made by numbers of 'royal' sons, who proved their parentage by the time-honoured 'ordeal by fire.' The technical side of warming up the metal was in the hands of the priesthood, who varied the heat according to their appreciation of the claimant, which was usually the same thing as the supposed appreciation of the claimant for the clergy!

Magnus, the son of Sigurd Jorsalafarer, was obviously the rightful monarch, so it was necessary for the next claimant to mutilate him by blinding and other bestialities. He was then shut up in a monastery in 1134, to be known henceforth as '*King Magnus the Blind.*'

In 1135 yet another claimant to royal parentage arose in Sigurd Slembe who, in 1136, succeeded in murdering the torturer of

Magnus the Blind—King Harald Gille. But Sigurd could not obtain support for his claims in Trondheim, so abstracted poor mutilated Magnus from his monastery there and both eventually arrived in Denmark.

In the summer of 1138 Magnus the Blind and Sigurd Slembe returned to Norway with a fleet of seven ships, three of which sailed on in wild flight to Haalogaland after King Inge's supporters had surprised them down south. Magnus the Blind spent the winter on Bjarkøy with his aged foster-father Vidkunn Jonson, who must then have been over seventy years of age. It seems that old Vidkunn could not have approved of Sigurd Slembe and refused to give him asylum at Bjarkøy. For Sigurd sunk his vessel at Øksfjord ($68\frac{1}{4}°$) on the south side of Hinnøy, took up winter quarters in a hole on a mountainside in 'Gljufrafjordr,' and hung 'something' in front of the entrance so that they could not be seen from the opposite shore. This fjord is thought to be the modern Gullesfjord, and a hole answering the saga description was still there until a landslide covered it in about 1870. The head of Gullesfjord would have been a splendid place to avoid detection, whilst escape from it was possible in several directions—and Bjarkøy was not far away.

The saga relates that Sigurd Slembe caused the Lapps to build him two vessels at the head of the fjord, whose planks were held together with gut. No nails were used, willow wands formed the ribs, and twelve men rowed on each side. These Haalogaland boats sailed so fast that none could overhaul them—'the sinew-bound ships sway under the sail,' as is stated in an ancient lay.

Sigurd lived with the Lapps whilst the boats were building, and they brewed beer and arranged feasts for him. Sigurd composed a song himself, in which:

It was good to be in the gammen (turf-hut) where we drank joyfully, and the king's son walked happily between the benches. Fun was not lacking at the cheerful drinking-feasts and we amused each other whilst I was there.

In the spring of 1139 Sigurd and poor Magnus went south with the two Lapp boats. They landed at Vaagan and slew the priest and his two sons. Then they sailed south to Vik in Brønnøy where they captured and killed the King's Lieutenant, Viljam Skinnare, presumably a descendant of Ketil Krog from Torghatten. Having plundered all along the coasts of Norway they sailed across to Denmark, whence they returned in the autumn of the same year, with Danish reinforcements, to meet their fates. As the mutilated Magnus drew his last breath he is reported to have said: 'This has come seven years too late,' whilst Sigurd Slembe died under indescribable tortures.

In 1153 the Pope sent the Englishman—Cardinal Nicholas Breakespeare (later Pope Adrian IV)—to Norway to put the affairs of the Church in order. The saga states that 'he made many improvements in the customs of the Norwegians whilst he was in the country': and we know from other sources that he founded the hierarchy and cathedral chapters to elect the bishops, whilst he gave Norway its first Archbishopric at Nidaros (Trondheim) and thereby made the Church of Norway independent. It is not known whether Breakespeare's mission had any echo in Haalogaland, but it is thought that the first stone church at Alstahaug (66°) was erected about the time of his visit, whilst that on the near-by island of South Herøy is known to be one of the oldest stone churches in Norway.

In these troublous times it was *Nicholas Skjaldvorson* of Steigen—the son of Sigurd Raneson—who wielded most power in Haalogaland. He was 'lieutenant' and had 'finneferd,' but resided mostly at Trondheim where he had a fine hall. He fought with King Haakon Haardebred at the Battle of Konghelle (1159), but turned his coat after defeat and became one of King Inge's most zealous adherents. When Inge died in 1161 there was talk of making Nicholas leader of the 'lieutenants' in all Norway, but he recommended that some member of the royal house be chosen.

When the renowned *Erling Skakke* later seized power he intrigued that his own son *Magnus Erlingson* become king, and those two had Nicholas as their most influential and active supporter in North and Central Norway. In the ensuing struggles that King Magnus and his father had with various other pretenders to the throne, Nicholas clung to the former, and when the rebel 'birch-legs' surprised Trondheim in 1176 they killed him in his dwelling there. Many sorrowed throughout North Norway, since the saga states that he was a noble and generous overlord.

It was under Erling Skakke and his son King Magnus Erlingson that the 'lieutenants' and bishops throughout Norway arrogated all authority to themselves. Royal power, as established by Harald Fairhair 300 years previously, had dwindled to a cipher, but in 1179 the Battle of Kalvskinnet (Trondheim) was won by Sverre and his 'birch-legs.' After a long struggle they re-established the centralized power of the Crown, and introduced a class of Civil Servants to administer its decrees throughout the length and breadth of Norway. Nicholas' son Sigurd fell at 'Kalvskinnet' together with Erling Skakke.

King Sverre (1179–1202)

It seems to have been in 1182 that Sverre sent a follower named Thorgils up to the most northern 'ting' district in Haalogaland to act as 'sysselman' and to conduct 'finneferd.' It is not stated whether Haalogaland had at that time submitted to Sverre, but most of the aristocrats would surely have stood out against him since his policy was to centralize authority under the Crown. The most influential family in Haalogaland was that at Bjarkøy, they being descendants in the female line of old Tore Hund. The representatives were the eighteen-year-old Vidkunn Erlingson and his two beautiful sisters, and when King Magnus heard that Vidkunn had inherited he summoned him to his presence, ostensibly to appoint him his 'lieutenant.' But gossip had it that the intention was either that Vidkunn should marry Magnus' sister Ragnhild, or else that Magnus wanted one of the Bjarkøy girls for himself.

Vidkunn promised to prove his loyalty to Magnus by clearing the 'birch-legs' from the Haalogaland fjords. Meanwhile Sverre's sysselman Thorgils spent the winter in the hinterland collecting Lapp-tax, and had assembled a fair parcel of furs, etc., which he accompanied southwards to take to Sverre. Vidkunn ambushed

Thorgils off Øksfjord ($68\frac{1}{2}°$) on his way south, killed him and all his men, and took the booty to Bjarkøy.

In the following spring Vidkunn left home in his forty-oared vessel *Gullringen*, that had formerly belonged to Archbishop Øiestein (Augustine) of Trondheim. Both his sisters accompanied him on King Magnus' invitation. The vessel was armed, and accompanied by a store-ship, but no one anticipated any hostile activity and so all weapons were stowed below the thwarts. But Sverre had received intelligence of Vidkunn's intentions, and sent seven ships to avenge Thorgils. On a May morning in 1183 Vidkunn's vessels were sighted north of Engeløy (68°). Sverre's boats at once crept behind 'Steigberget,' which is surely the promontory just north of Steigen Church on Engeløy. Vidkunn's ships did not observe them until they were at close quarters when they at once hauled their sail down. But the 'birch-legs' attacked instantaneously and Vidkunn's men had no time even to launch their small boat and send the women away. They had no shields or armour, merely spears and axes, and so the 'birch-legs' quickly gained the upper hand. Vidkunn himself was killed together with most of his crew, and *Gullringen* captured with all its contents. When the victors reached Trondheim Sverre was delighted, and it seems Vidkunn's sisters fell into his hands. He probably did not release them until King Magnus had fallen (1184), since he would not have run the risk that that king or one of his associates might have married them and thus acquired the valuable estates of the dead Vidkunn. One of these girls named Ragna later married Bjarne Maardson who was celebrated for his knowledge of law. It appears they returned to Bjarkøy to live.

At Sverre's great victory in the Battle of Fimreite (Sogn) in 1184 King Magnus Erlingson perished, and by his side fell Viljam of Torghatten, Anders Skjaldvorson of Tilrem (a son of Sigurd Raneson), and Ketil Fluga of Tjøtta. Thus the ranks of Haalogaland aristocracy were thinning out due to their opposition to Sverre and his 'birch-legs.' Bjarne Maardson of Bjarkøy joined the anti-Sverre Party known as 'bagler'—('Bishop's crook'—to give the impression that a bishop was their leader)—when they came to Haalogaland in force in 1198. They visited every fjord and plundered ruthlessly, thereby collecting much booty and attracting the best men in the province. But in 1199 King Sverre sent a strong force north, and Bjarne Maardson together with other adherents of the 'bagler' were heavily fined for their hostile activities.

Sverre put an end to the rule of the 'lieutenants' and ecclesiastics, and gave the perquisites that his enemies had enjoyed to his own followers, whilst at the same time linking them firmly to the Crown. Some became 'sysselmen' (king's local agents) and others 'lagmen' (men-of-law) to advise the peasantry on law and justice. Such a 'lag-man' did Sverre appoint for Haalogaland with headquarters at Steigen, where, on the flat island of Engeløy, the 'man of law' dispensed justice for 600 years, until the office was abolished in 1797. Steigen was no doubt selected by Sverre as being the most ancient centre in Haalogaland and the seat of the time-honoured Steigarting. Also Sigurd Raneson's former property there became Crown lands, after the 'birch-legs' had killed both his son and grandson in their battles at Trondheim.

King Sverre fought Pope and Church until the Crown gained the ascendancy, and the kingdom of Norway was acknowledged to be hereditary in his family.

The Civil War—final phase (1203–40)

Sverre's son Haakon ended the bitter quarrel between Crown and Church by concluding a truce that endured, but strife between the 'birch-legs' and 'bagler' continued for many years.

King Haakon Sverreson died (possibly poisoned) in 1204, leaving behind an unborn son who was to become the saviour of Norway. During his infancy, however, there was a surfeit of pretenders to the throne that kept Norway in a ferment.

The history of Haalogaland is a blank during the early years of the thirteenth century, but we do know that Viking activities were fostered by the unsettled state of Norway, including that notorious raid on the Hebrides in 1214 when even the island of Iona was sacked, a sacred spot that the crude Vikings had spared 250 years earlier.

In 1217 the thirteen-year-old Haakon Haakonson was acclaimed king, but a rival claimant arose in *Earl Skule*, whose ambitions kept the Civil War smouldering. So young Haakon agreed in 1219 to affiance himself to Margaret, the infant daughter of Skule, and hopes of internal peace were thereby revived. Haakon did all in his power to win Skule over, giving him the title of 'Duke' and control of Northern Norway.

In 1218 King Haakon appointed the respected Paal Vaagaskalm his 'lieutenant' at Dønnes (66°). He appears to have been previously 'sysselman' in Alstahaug where he was king's agent in Helgeland, but now became Lord-Lieutenant over the whole province. He was himself a Haalogalander, his family having been long settled at Vaagan in Lofoten.

In 1224 Duke Skule, together with Sigurd Ribbung (another pretender to the throne) travelled up to Haalogaland, possibly with the intention of being acclaimed king in that remote part that was already under his control but which he had probably never visited. Skule attended the 'trade-fair' at Vaagan and anchored in Kirkevaag (near Kabelvaag). Some of his followers murdered a nephew of Paal Vaagaskalm one evening, and when the Duke woke next morning he hurried ashore clad only in his underclothes to find the deed had been done. Paal Vaagaskalm had arrived during the night, summoned a 'ting' and would not consent to reconciliation.

After Duke Skule had touched the shrine of St. Olav in Trondheim and taken the title of 'King' in 1239, he sent emissaries up to Haalogaland. One went overland and the other two up the 'Inner Lead,' assassinating all whom they believed to be supporters of King Haakon. The King's sysselmen and his followers sought refuge in the church at Sandnes one evening in hope of sanctuary, but the Duke's bandits (known as 'varbelger') threatened to burn down the church. Guthorm, the sysselman, then left it on the assurance that St. Olav's peace would be kept, but he was murdered and his vessel seized.

Then the 'varbelger' killed the King's men on Traena and at Medalbu near Gildeskaal, and so to Salten and Leines. They got no farther, since the King's sysselman at Hamarøy hastily manned seven vessels which arrived at Leines at daybreak. They seized one of the 'varbelger' boats whilst the remainder fled to Trondheim. Duke Skule upbraided them for denying sanctuary and for killing Guthorm, but he none the less annexed the major portion of the booty.

No rising of the masses in favour of Duke Skule took place either in Haalogaland or elsewhere. Only a small section of the aristocracy supported him, amongst whom was Viljam of Torghatten who could not forget that an ancestor had fallen fighting against King Sverre. Duke Skule was killed at Elgesaeter Abbey in Trondheim in May 1240, and with his fall ended the disastrous Civil War that had persisted for 109 years.

A happy and prosperous era dawned for all Norway.

The latter years of King Haakon Haakonson (1240–63)

After the close of the Civil War the remainder of the reign of Haakon Haakonson was a brilliant period in Norway's history. He lived at peace with the Church, and the Crown took over all authority formerly wielded by the aristocrats.

There was still great wealth in Haalogaland amongst the plutocratic families, many of which were offshoots of the famous Bjarkøy stock. But the King's Civil Servants now took control in the country districts, they being rewarded with Crown lands for the services they had rendered to the King.

The new sense of security induced pious and wealthy men to erect stone churches, of which the finest example still stands at *Trondenes* near Harstad. Gothic in design and dated about 1250, it stands on a promontory with fjords and islands all around. It had two towers as late as early eighteenth century but these have now vanished. The existing stone church is thought to have replaced a wooden one built by King Øiestein in about 1110, which did duty for 150 years. With an increase of population the wooden church became too small, so the stone chancel was added to it, and the nave at some later date still. It is not known who the builder was, but Audun Raude was priest here for a long while before being elevated to the bishopric of Holar on

Iceland, where he evidenced great interest in church construction. Around the old church runs a defensive work which in places is 15 feet in height. In the wall to seaward, near the gable of the chancel, were two watch-towers, the whole forming a strong position. This wall round the church and churchyard is perhaps the oldest piece of work, and possibly dates from 1110. It was extended and improved in about 1250, the enemy in those days being the Kvens (Finlanders) and Karelians who ravaged the northern frontier districts. Trondenes Church bears a resemblance to Trondheim Cathedral and must have been built in an era of prosperity and by men with knowledge and foresight. It has stood through the ages as an unique monument from Haalogaland's flowering period.

Lenvik Church (Gisundet—$69\frac{1}{4}°$) was until about 1250 the most northerly in the country, it being used by the people of North Malangen and still farther north. But then King Haakon erected a church on Troms Island (undoubtedly where the cathedral now stands), and in the saga we read:—

King Haakon did more to fortify Christianity in Norway than any king before him since St. Olav. He built a church in the north at *Troms* and Christianized the whole parish. Many Bjarmer came to him, who had fled from the east for fear of the Tartars. He christened them and gave them a fjord called *Malangen*. He also built a church in Ofoten. [This latter was probably at Evenes.]

It seems probable that the purpose of Troms Island church was for missionary work amongst those who had not accepted Christianity, i.e. the Lapps, but how much truth there is in the saga account cannot be determined. It is, however, certain that Haakon built the church, and in the following century it still bore the name of '*Mariakirk juxta paganos*.' There are numerous evidences of Norse occupation far north of Tromsø from the Viking period and eleventh century. A find of silver on Skjervøy ($70°$) from the middle of the eleventh century, included coins of Canute the Great and a crucifix and figure of Christ. If we believe the saga story then the Norsemen must have retreated south in the twelfth–thirteenth centuries, but from other evidence we possess this seems most improbable. It is also known that King Haakon

54

had 'sysselmen' to the north in Finnmark who came into collision with the bailiffs of *Novgorod*, but there is no indication that the Mongol invasion of what is now Russia reached so far north as to cause the Bjarmer (Karelians) to flee. What is certain is that from about 1220 there was an end to 'Bjarmelandsferder,' and at the same time the consolidation of the Norwegian frontiers to the north and east was undertaken seriously.

The church on Troms Isle was one of the fourteen Royal chapels in Norway, to which the King himself nominated the priests—the Cathedral Chapter of Trondheim had little or no property up north. It was sited at a strategical spot, whence the missionaries could safely roam at large over the scattered islands and fjords. Crusades were in fashion in Haakon's days, and the Pope implored him to lead one. Haakon refused—perhaps because he had his hands full spreading Christianity in his own country.

There is a fortification from the Middle Ages at Tromsø called 'Skansen' to this day, which may date from Haakon Haakonson's time. Situated on a point a little north of the harbour it gave better protection than if placed close to the church. For economic reasons also the church had to be sited on Tromsø Sound, since all the through-traffic to Finnmark passed that way, and it drew its revenue from the traders.

Another ancient church in Haalogaland is at Dønnes (66°), which Paal Vaagaskalm surely built as his private chapel in the thirteenth century. Prior to its restoration in 1866 it consisted only of a nave, had very thick walls and a fine Norman stone door. It is the only one of the very few private chapels erected in North Norway that is still standing. Two other churches from the time of Haakon Haakonson are at South Herøy (66°) and Gildeskaal, whilst a part of Alstahaug may date from about 1150.

King Haakon Haakonson died in 1263 at Kirkwall in the Orkneys, at the close of his celebrated campaign against Scotland that ended with the Battle of Largs.

Magnus the 'Law-Improver' and his sons (1263–1319)

The first act of Magnus Lagabøter was to make peace with Scotland by the Treaty of Perth in 1266, one of the negotiators being Paal Vaagaskalm of Dønnes. By this treaty the sovereignty of the Hebrides and Man passed to Scotland, though those islands remained within the Diocese of Trondheim until the Reformation. Today there is a Bishop of 'Sodor and Man'— (Syderøer=Hebrides)—in the hierarchy of the Church of England.

Magnus unified the ancient provincial laws into one national code which became valid throughout Norway. In effecting this, however, he met with opposition from the bishops, who were loth to have their temporal authority weakened.

In 1263 *Erling Ivarson* of Bjarkøy is mentioned as being 'King's Lieutenant' in Haalogaland, and the following year he gave some property there to the church at Bjarkøy. He had two sons— Vidkunn and Bjarne—who, partly owing to fortunate marriages, became the wealthiest and most influential men in Norway. They were both honoured with the title of 'baron,' a rank which was instituted in 1277 by King Magnus, as also that of 'ridder' (knight).

Vidkunn Erlingson lived mostly at Bjarkøy, where was born to him in 1292 a son who became renowned as *Erling Vidkunnson*.

Bjarne Erlingson was born about 1250, and married the wealthiest heiress in all Norway. When King Magnus died in 1280 he was made President of the Regency to the two young sons of Magnus—Erik and Haakon. Bjarne took up the cudgels against the bishops who excommunicated him, but Bjarne won and the Archbishop vanished into Sweden, leaving his throne at Trondheim vacant during six years. In the summer of 1282 Bjarne held a 'ting' at Bruberge, near Storvaagan in Lofoten, where the so-called 'Vaagabok' was declared illegal. It was a code of laws for Vaagan and the fisheries there and had clauses determining tithes. Bjarne stated that the King would permit but one law-book in Norway and 'nessekonger' (local kinglets) would not be tolerated. Audun Raude of Trondenes and a brother priest refused to comply and were heavily fined, whilst, incidentally, Bjarne vetoed the custom of parents giving salt and wax to the church when a child was baptized.

When the young kings Erik and Haakon took over the reins of government they agreed to some form of reconciliation with the bishops, and things looked bad for Bjarne when he was summoned to appear at the Archbishop's Court in 1291 to account for his actions in Lofoten ten years previously. But Bjarne absented himself, and the Archbishop had the depositions of witnesses taken down on a parchment that is still in existence. No further action was taken, however, since the Archbishop wanted peace with the leading men in the country, so the excommunication of Bjarne and his associates was immediately lifted.

In 1281 Bjarne Erlingson led an embassy to Scotland in the matter of the marriage of the young King Erik to Princess Margaret. In 1284 he went to England as ambassador, whilst the following year he and his brother Vidkunn went on an embassy to Denmark and Sweden. In 1286–87 he was again in Scotland, and later took an active part in the negotiations with Scotland and England as to the future of 'Pigen fra Norge' (the *Maid of Norway*). Margaret, Queen of Norway and Princess of Scotland, had scarcely closed her eyes when her only brother Alexander died suddenly. It was then clear that Margaret, her little daughter by King Erik, would eventually succeed to the throne of Scotland. In 1289 representatives from Norway, Scotland and England met at Salisbury and agreed she be sent to Scotland as its rightful Queen. It was later arranged that she should marry the son of Edward I of England. As is well known 'Pigen fra Norge' died in the Orkneys in 1290, and with her died also the dreams of a 'Union of North Sea Powers' in the fourteenth century.

For forty years Bjarne Erlingson was the leading figure in Norway in all negotiations and campaigns, in drafting of laws and confirming judgments. As late as 1312–13 he was the leader of an important embassy to the King of Scotland. He is also remembered for his literary interests, and when Ambassador to Scotland in 1286–87 he acquired a copy of *The Life of Charlemagne*, a part of which he had translated into Norwegian. Amidst his manifold activities he never forgot his ancestral home at Bjarkøy, and in his will dated 1309 he left considerable sums to the church there. To a sister-in-law he left the gold belt 'which the Great Edward, King of England, gave to me.'

Bjarne died in 1313 and was buried in Trondheim Cathedral, leaving as heir his nephew *Erling Vidkunnson* who was to become so famous.

For so long as Trondheim was the capital of Norway, Haalogaland lay near the country's heart. But little by little the centre of gravity moved south and east, and as early as 1272 we read: 'the northern districts are now less populous.' Migration to Eastern Norway was considerable in the twelfth and thirteenth centuries, and many an aristocratic family also moved eastwards. When King *Haakon V* made Oslo the capital in 1286, had himself crowned there in 1299 and built Akershus fortress in 1300, Haalogaland indeed became a distant province. But it seems the King did not forget it since he is said to have remarked: 'Come let us take care of Haalogaland since it lies so far away.' He promulgated new laws in respect of the Lapps in 1313, by which the Norwegians were to take care of them and no longer plague them with extortions. He tempted the Lapps to embrace Christianity by exempting those that did so from taxation for twenty years.

In 1319 died Haakon V Magnusson, and with him Harald Fairhair's male line petered out after ruling Norway for 450 years. He left an only daughter Ingeborg, and a long period of dynastic union with Sweden began.

Trade and Commerce in the Thirteenth Century

In the very-long-ago the export trade of North Norway was in the hands of Norwegian traders who sailed direct for England, or to Bergen as entrepot for fish from the north. But English traders began visiting Bergen and soon gained the mastery, their activities being encouraged by King Sverre and the famous 'Treaty of Free Trade' between the two countries concluded in 1217. As late as 1260 the trade with England dominated, but the 1280's mark a turning-point in the commercial history of Northern Europe owing to the rapid rise in power of the Hansa merchants. This was particularly the case in the Baltic lands whose corn was in such demand in Haalogaland, and the Norwegians were squeezed out of their former trading routes.

The export articles from Bergen included goat and sheepskins, whale-fat and cod-liver oil, furs, falcons, sulphur, tar, etc. But the largest article of export was dried fish (stokkfish) and herring from Haalogaland. The English trade was the lifeline of Norwegian shipping, which could not acquiesce without demur in permitting all the stokkfish from Bergen to be carried in German bottoms to the German warehouses at Boston in Lincolnshire and elsewhere. So in 1282 Germans were precluded from buying goods for export during the winter months unless they had brought flour, malt or rye to Norway.

But then war broke out with the Hanseatic League, which did its best to starve Norway into submission. All the ports from Reval to Ghent were closed, trade with England alone being possible. It was Bjarne Erlingson who negotiated peace with the Hansa in 1294, they acquiring the right to trade with Norway but not to sail north of Bergen. The Hansa succeeded in stifling all competition in Bergen and this was fatal to Norwegian overseas traders. The ensuing economic depression hit Norwegians badly, but North Norway prospered for a time, owing to the rise in fish prices which the widespread Hansa markets brought about.

Finnmark—from earliest times to the Treaty of Novgorod (1326)

The territory constituting the modern province of Finnmark differs so greatly from ancient Haalogaland as to physical features, the racial characteristics of its inhabitants, and its political and commercial histories, that it requires a section of its own in this volume.

All down the centuries fishing and hunting have provided its people with their means of livelihood, whilst cultivation and forestry have scarcely been operated.

Tacitus called 'The People beyond Scandinavia, Fenni'—and Ptolemy, 'finnoi.' 'Finns' is the oldest Scandinavian name for the natives and is used by Norwegians to this day, whilst they call themselves 'samer.' The word 'Lappia' is used by Saxo (1200), and the Swedes still call them 'Lapps,' even as do the British.

One must differentiate between mountain-Lapps and forest-Lapps. The former own reindeer which cannot tolerate mosquitoes or the heat of summertime, at which season they either wander into the hills above the mosquito-line or swim across to the off-lying islands. The reindeer of the forest-Lapps have become accustomed to both mosquitoes and heat, and hence the forest-Lapps are not so nomadic.

The Lapps had to pay for the right to live in peace in Norwegian Finnmark by submitting to the form of taxation imposed upon them. Ottar says that in the ninth century they were subject to Norwegian chieftains in Haalogaland, 'paid tribute and had for long done so.' When Harald Fairhair united Norway in 872 he made trading with the Lapps and their taxation a royal monopoly, and appointed some favourite supporter his agent to collect it on journeys that were called 'finneferd.' Torolv Kveldulvson's 'finneferd' in 877 was among the forest-Lapps in what is now North Sweden, whilst Karle and Gunnstein's 'finneferd' in 1026 was by long-ship on the coasts of modern Finnmark. Ottar's account hints at an ancient and much traversed route to the East—the so-called 'Bjarmelandsferd.' Erik Bloody-Axe and Harald Graafeld fought with the Bjarmer and plundered them.

Historia Norvegiae (1170) states that Vegestav was the coastal boundary between Norway and Bjarmeland. Vegestav seems to have been the ancient name for Svjatoi Nos (Helgenes) which is mentioned in 1730 as being the former eastern limit of Norwegian territory. This is the extreme eastern point of the Kola Peninsula at the entrance to the White Sea. Hence all the coast known today as 'Murmansk' was then part of Norway—indeed the Russians still call it 'Murmanska Sembla' (the Northmen's Country) and the sea 'Murmanske Muri' (the Northmen's Sea).

The Norwegians always maintained that unoccupied Finnmark was their territory, and they exacted tribute from other peoples who wished to live or wander there. That they, as lords of the land, had hunting rights was a matter of course, and this was the practice in Ottar's time, at all events as far as the North Cape, especially in search of walrus. As the centuries passed unoccupied Finnmark became much reduced in area owing to districts being absorbed by Norwegians, Swedes, Kvens (Finlanders) and Karelians, so that many of the districts where Lapps wandered in Ottar's time are no longer available to their successors. Ottar's account is the oldest and most reliable that we have of conditions in Finnmark eleven centuries ago.

In earliest times the Lapps were the sole occupants of Finnmark but other peoples were tempted there by its natural wealth. The Norwegians were the first to find their way there, and then came the Russians from the east—raiding at first and later to trade. Lastly the 'Kvens' wandered in from their forests north of the Gulf of Bothnia and pioneered in Finnmark, where there was always food in the shape of fish from the sea to keep body and soul together when famine stalked elsewhere. And so Finnmark became a meeting-place for four races, and this mixture stamps social life up there to this very day.

Just because Finnmark was a 'no man's land' its position was unique politically, since it was essential for the King of Norway to assert his rights there. From being a 'no man's land' it became the personal property of the King—a state of affairs that was frequently contested by neighbouring powers, but finally admitted in the frontier agreements of 1751 and 1826. The right to trade in Finnmark became a royal privilege in early days, and the King might at times delegate his authority to others but never lost sight of his perquisites.

As late as the twelfth century there were no Norwegians actually settled in Finnmark. They visited it to acquire furs and the products of the Arctic Ocean, but did not spend the winters so far north. Gulating Law commands the Haalogalanders to arm ships 'as they have guard duties towards the east.'

In 1238 some Bjarmer fled from Mongol terror and subjected themselves to Norway's king, he giving them land at Malangen.

In 1251 an embassy from Novgorod to King Haakon Haakonson complained of clashes between the King's agents and the East Karelians in northern Finnmark. A Norwegian embassy returned to Novgorod to conclude a peace between the two countries and their tributary lands. This is the earliest treaty between Norway and Russia, but the original no longer exists.

Icelandic annals report a plunder raid in 1271, carried out by Kvens and Karelians on northern Haalogaland, and in 1279 they captured the 'sysselman' there and killed thirty-five of his men in the mountains when collecting taxes. These attacks were repeated in 1302.

There must have been several Norwegians resident in the coastal outposts in 1307, in which year the Archbishop of Trondheim himself went to Vardø to consecrate a church, whilst in the same year the fortress of Vardøhus was erected.

After the Hansa merchants were granted their Bergen privileges in 1294, the Lofoten catch no longer sufficed to satisfy the demand their widespread European markets created. The price of fish rose, and more and more Norwegians went to Finnmark to fish—and so commenced the famous 'Finnmark Fisheries.' But at about the same time, the Hansa took over the Russian fur trade using Novgorod as its chief centre. Hence the Norwegian fur trade dwindled whilst its fish trade multiplied. The fish was shipped to Vaagan (Lofoten) where Norwegian merchants bought it and transported it in Norwegian bottoms to Bergen, since the Hansa merchants were expressly forbidden to sail north of that port.

In 1313 the Lapps were reported as being in a sorry plight owing to 'squeezes' by Norwegians and Karelians, and in 1316 Russians attacked Haalogaland and killed many Norwegians. Vatican letters show that Karelian and Russian plunder-raids increased after the death of King Haakon V in 1319, and 'that the heathen Lapps joined them.' In 1319 the Crowns of Norway and Sweden were united, but when the Peace of Nöteborg (Schlüsselberg) was concluded between Sweden and Novgorod in 1323 there was no mention of Norway, so hostilities continued there. In that year of 1323 the Karelian-Russians penetrated Haalogaland so far as to burn down Erling Vidkunnson's ancestral home on Bjarkøy.

On June 3, 1326, the Peace of Novgorod was signed between the plenipotentiary of Magnus Erikson, King of Norway and Sweden, on the one hand, 'and all Novgorod's inhabitants.' The ancient frontiers were to be respected but these were, however, not defined. The original of the treaty is lost, but a copy has been preserved which shows that in 1326 Novgorod recognized Finnmark as being Norwegian territory. That there was no mention of frontier marks in the treaty was surely because none knew where it ran, except for the existence of Vegestav that was purely a coastal frontier point. The Norwegian authorities failed to delimit any fixed frontier, and were content to recognize vast *common districts* in which both Norwegians and Russians could collect tribute from the Lapps.

And so commenced, with a vague definition, the vexed question of the 'common districts' in Finnmark that caused such difficulties at highest levels during the ensuing centuries.

PART III

FROM THE FIRST UNION (1319) to the REFORMATION (1536)

Haalogaland during the Fourteenth Century

WHEN the male line of the family of Harald Fairhair died out in 1319 the leading figure in Norway was without question *Erling Vidkunnson*, then aged twenty-seven, having been born at Bjarkøy in 1292. He inherited rich estates in the north and west of Norway from his father and uncle, and acquired by marriage vast properties in East Norway and in the far-distant Orkneys. It was Norway's good fortune at this critical period in her history to find a leader of such integrity and outstanding qualities as Erling Vidkunnson.

A little boy, *Magnus Erikson*, inherited the throne in 1319 from his grandfather Haakon V, through a mother the Princess Ingeborg, who seems to have abused such powers as came her way. She chose adventurers as her advisers, one of whom, Knut Porse, became her lover and eventual husband. The Norwegians did not in any event appreciate being ruled by a woman, and so, at a National Meeting in Oslo (1323), Erling Vidkunnson was chosen to be Viceroy and Lord High Constable. Those offices gave him royal powers in finance, defence and justice. He controlled the governance of the entire country on the advice and with the agreement of the Council of State. Through his mother he was related to the Royal Family, and bore for his coat-of-arms a lion rampant gripping a gold-hilted sword with its right forepaw.

Judging from the slender sources available Norway was well governed during the nine years he held office, but there were several difficulties to cope with, including hostilities with Russia. Karelians raided Haalogaland in 1323 and burnt Erling's home

3. Trondenes Church, built *c.* 1250

4. Chancel door of Alstahaug Church from *c.* 1150

on Bjarkøy, after which the Swedes induced the Pope to proclaim a crusade against the heathens. These Russian troubles were an off-shoot of the frontier war between Sweden and Novgorod over Karelia, and in a sense were the first misfortunes that befell Norway owing to its dynastic union with Sweden.

Erling appealed to the Pope in 1324, sending two Frenchmen who were in his service to Avignon to obtain authority to levy taxes on the Norwegian clergy. Erling also appealed directly to the Archbishop for: 'the assistance of all Norway to defend Haalogaland against the enemies of God—Lapps, Russians and Karelians.' The hierarchy refused, whereupon Erling sent an embassy to Novgorod that negotiated a ten-year peace. This agreement of 1326 exists in a law book that appears to have been Erling's personal property, and is of great interest as being the earliest frontier agreement between Norway and Russia.

Erling did all in his power to help Haalogaland in matters of trade, and took up the quarrel with the Hansa in Bergen whilst pressing a national policy in commerce.

When King Magnus came of age in 1332 and assumed royal powers in both Norway and Sweden, Erling gave up his office but continued as the leading figure in the State. King Magnus spent most of his time in Sweden, and Erling was the moving spirit in the demand for an independent Council of State. In 1339 the leading Norwegians held a meeting at Tønsberg, at which they drafted demands on King Magnus that included improvement of certain fortresses, among which was that of Vardø. In 1340 Erling and the Archbishop made arrangements for minting the coinage, and in 1343 a decree was issued that Haakon, the youngest son of Magnus, should become King of Norway whilst his elder brother should succeed to the throne of Sweden. The signatures to that decree include Erling Vidkunnson and his son Bjarne Erlingson.

Erling survived the 'Black Death' in 1349 and went to Rome in 1350. On his way home it seems certain he became a prisoner of the English, since the later 'Domesday Book' of Archbishop Aslak Bolt states that Archbishop Olav (Erling's contemporary) acquired both Tjøtta and Tilrem from Erling Vidkunnson in return for the gold and silver he had expended when Erling was a prisoner in England.

Erling Vidkunnson died in 1355, aged sixty-three, and it seems probable that he was the last notable figure to live at Bjarkøy, which had again been raided by Karelians in 1349. The grand estate was kept together for a time, but Bjarkøy had lost its former importance—the chief cause probably being that trade with the White Sea ended once the Hansa merchants had established the centre of their fur trade at Novgorod.

Erling Vidkunnson had only one son *Bjarne Erlingson* (the younger), who was born in 1315. He played a very small part in the history of North Norway since Tønsberg and Bergen were the centres of his activities. He died childless in 1353—two years before his father.

The Black Death (1349)

An Icelandic account states:

A ship arrived from England with a large crew and anchored at Vaagen in Bergen. Only a small part of the cargo had been unloaded when everybody on board died, and when the goods that had been landed reached the city many inhabitants perished immediately. Thence the infection spread all over Norway. . . .

Haalogaland suffered severely, as can be seen in Archbishop Aslak Bolt's 'Domesday Book' of 1434—indeed some estimates put the death roll at 66 per cent of its population. This plague of 1349 was followed by others in 1359 and 1371, and it was a decimated and poverty-stricken Haalogaland that fished its seas and turned its soil. The clergy were the greatest sufferers as they caught the infection when administering the last rites, and with them dwindled such culture as there was in the North in the fourteenth century. The Black Death brought but one good result, in that it reached Novgorod and induced that Power to make a peace with Norway in 1351 that endured till 1385.

Hansa Trade in Haalogaland

In the Norway–Hansa Treaty of 1294 it was laid down that no non-Norwegian should sail north of Bergen. This provision was reaffirmed in 1306, was contravened, and had to be reasserted in 1348. During the first half of the fourteenth century Vaagan in Lofoten was the entrepot for all the fish of North Norway, and from there merchants of Norwegian nationality transported the catch to Bergen. Then came 'The Black Death' to paralyse the Norwegian merchants and open the gate to the monopoly of the Hansa merchants resident in Bergen. They began regular sailing north of Bergen in spite of the prohibition, and when the sysselmen up north endeavoured to put obstacles in their way they complained to the King. He was obliged to be careful in his dealings with the Hansa, who were at that time indispensable as being the sole suppliers of corn to West and North Norway. In a decree of 1361 the King gave all 'native merchants' (including the Germans domiciled in Bergen) permission to travel north and south and to the tributary lands with their merchandise.

It profited nothing that certain kings endeavoured to restrict the trade of the Hansa. In 1384 King Olav VI decreed that natives of Haalogaland and Finnmark were no more to sail to the cities of the south with their fish, but take their produce to Vaagan in Lofoten where citizens of Bergen were now permitted to travel and trade. The reason given for this decree was that: 'since Karelians and Russians have broken the peace with the men of Norway' the Haalogalanders were to remain at home to defend themselves when the Russians came. But its purpose seems actually to have been to check a trade development and return to ancient practices. In this it failed, and so the merchants of Bergen, including the Hansa ones, retained their rights to individual trade with the north. Although there were frequent disputes between the Norwegian Crown and the Hansa, it always ended in the privileges of the latter being confirmed and extended.

In addition to the more substantial merchants of Bergen there were numbers of smaller traders who were its citizens but spent the summer or all the year peddling their wares in Haalogaland. After the Black Death the Hansa left few opportunities for native Norwegians, who were reduced to the status of peddlars.

The 'Union of Kalmar' (1397)

From about 1350 Haakon, the son of Magnus Erikson, ruled in Norway, but Magnus remained titular king until his death by drowning in 1374. Six years later King Haakon VI died, leaving his widow the renowned Margaret as Norway's ruler. Following the death of her little son Olav in 1387 she was chosen as ruler by both Danes and Norwegians, and in 1397 the 'Union of Kalmar' placed the crowns of all three Scandinavian countries upon the one head of her sister's grandson Erik of Pommern. There was to be no question of any *primus inter pares* between the three kingdoms, their equality in all matters being carefully laid down. In such manner did the fourteenth century come to its close.

From the Union of Kalmar to the Reformation (1397–1536)

By the dawn of the fifteenth century the ravages of the Black Death had somewhat spent themselves in Haalogaland, and the fact that the Hansa merchants had procured markets for its fish brought prosperity all along its coasts. Fishery in Lofoten and Finnmark became a considerable industry based on export, and districts such as Andenes, Langenes and various centres in Finnmark attracted a considerable population that had no concern with agriculture, and so was all the more dependent on fishing. The Germans brought flour, salt and hemp and returned with Norwegian dried fish (stokkfish).

A German colony settled in Bergen whose members dealt with individual fishermen in North Norway, and thus democratized the trade that the 'plutocrats' had formerly monopolized. Elsewhere in Norway the centuries between the close of the saga-period and the Reformation were ages of depression, but in Haalogaland and Finnmark it was quite otherwise, due to the enterprise and salesmanship of the Hanseatic fish merchants.

The English made a bid to trade with North Norway early in the fifteenth century. They had for long controlled the fisheries on Iceland and now extended their activities to Lofoten, Troms and Finnmark. There was a complaint to King Erik of Pommern in 1420 that two English ships had visited Troms and would return in greater numbers the following summer. In 1428 several English vessels visited Finnmark, but the sysselmen and people there gave them a warm reception and seized some of the traders.

The kings of England and Norway signed a treaty in 1432, a clause in which reads: 'the men and women whom the English have taken away from Iceland, Finnmark and Haalogaland' are to be set free and sent home, and be paid for the work they had done. The same treaty restates the old prohibition against foreign traders in Haalogaland, and reasserts that the entrepot for fish is to be Bergen, where the English have the same rights as the Germans. The purpose was of course to protect the fisheries of Lofoten and the traders in Haalogaland from foreign competition. English trading with North Norway was opened again by a treaty in 1489, but revoked by King Frederik I in 1524.

After King Christian I had confirmed the privileges of the Hansa in 1455, he also gave the citizens of Trondheim the right to trade anywhere in Norway. But Bergen remained the chief market for the fisheries of the north, due to the fact that the Hansa could ensure a good and regular supply of bread-grains. The former importation of corn and flour from England consisted mainly of wheat and wheaten-flour, but the fisheries created a considerable demand for cheaper varieties which the Hansa could always supply. Vast quantities of rye, besides wheat and other foodstuffs, were brought from the Baltic countries to satisfy the requirements of the coastal Norwegians. This was a blessed arrangement for North Norway through a couple of centuries. The disposal of fish and fish products was regular and assured whilst the price of flour and other foodstuffs was reasonably in proportion to that of fish, and as long as circumstances remained so favourable there was contentment and a good standard of living in the north.

But these two centuries laid the foundations for a system of trade that was to bring about fateful consequences for North Norway under less favourable circumstances.

There is a woeful lack of records from this period. Communications with Iceland were all but broken after the Black Death, and that island of noble skalds could no longer produce sagas depicting life in Norway. The educated 'plutocrats' in Haalogaland thinned out, largely owing to the change in economic conditions there due to the methods of the all-powerful Hansa, whilst the priesthood took a long time to re-estabish a cultural *niveau*. The one safe source is the 'Domesday Book' of Archbishop Aslak Bolt of Trondheim that was compiled in 1434. It gives a schedule of the properties of the Church and covers those in Haalogaland.

Aslak Bolt was a great-grandson of the renowned Erling Vidkunnson (died 1355), and was born about 1380. Queen Margaret appointed him Bishop of Bergen in 1408, where he evidenced considerable ability as administrator and organizer. He became Archbishop of Trondheim in 1428 and proceeded to bring order into the finances of the Diocese. His 'Domesday' makes it clear that there were few settlers up the fjords, whilst not a single dwelling is recorded that was more than two English miles from salt water. Out in the Lofotens, Vesteraalen and Senja, as also along the coast of Helgeland there was a considerable population. The largest settlements were at Andenes and Dverberg in Vesteraalen, where remains have been found of hundreds of boat-houses indicating their importance as centres of the fisheries.

The Italians on Røst (1432)

On the island of Røst ($67\frac{1}{2}°$), lying at the extreme tip of the Lofoten Archipelago, some destitute sailors landed early in 1432. Their vessel had been wrecked on a voyage from Crete to Flanders, and the survivors drifted north-east till they arrived at lonely Røst in varying degrees of exhaustion. When they had returned to their native Venice, Captain Quirini and his crew recorded their experiences whilst marooned on Røst. Quirini, who came of a good family and had seen a great deal of the world, drew comparisons between their Haalogaland hosts and his own countrymen that are of great value from so travelled a man. They provide a rare glimpse through the 'Iron Curtain,' behind which the people of North Norway lived through a long period.

There were 120 souls on the island who lived by the rich fisheries there, two kinds of cod (skrei and torsk) and halibut forming the bulk of the catch. From these they produced 'stokkfish' by drying them in the sun and wind till they were as hard as boards. They beat the 'stokkfish' before cooking it with butter and herbs, when it tasted delicious.

The men were clean in their persons, and they and their womenfolk good-looking. Their habits simple and trusting, for they did not lock doors at night and had full confidence in their women. This the Italians realized when the men went out fishing early leaving their women with them, for Quirini and his men slept in the same room as the men, their wives and daughters! They were practising Christians and attended Mass on Sundays and Saints' Days, whilst at Easter 72 out of the 120 took Communion. They never quarrelled or used bad language.

Their houses were of log-timbers with a vent in the roof for light and smoke, and this they covered with transparent fish-skin in the winter. To accustom children to the cold they laid four-day-old babes naked under the vent so that snow might fall upon them. Their clothes were of coarse cloth from England and elsewhere, and they seldom wore skins.

The Italians were given fresh milk daily, since each household possessed from four to six cows. 'We can truthfully say that from February 3rd until May 1432 we lived in Paradise, and they put Italian habits to shame'—so wrote the First Officer of the wrecked ship.

On May 14, 1432, they sailed away south in a Røst vessel bound for Bergen with dried fish, the island priest—a German monk—accompanied them. Near Brønnøy they met Archbishop Aslak Bolt on his way north touring his diocese. He gave the Italians a letter to the Cathedral Chapter in Trondheim, where they were hospitably entertained and re-equipped for their further wanderings. As war was on with the Hansa they did not return by sea but crossed into Sweden and so home to Venice overland.

In the summer of 1932 a memorial was unveiled on Røst to commemorate this event on its five hundredth anniversary.

The Dynasty

After the death of the great Queen Margaret in 1412 it became clear that Erik of Pommern would soon get himself into trouble. His English Queen, *Philippa*—a sister of Henry V of Agincourt —was definitely his 'better half.' There is no record that she ever visited Norway and she died at Vadstena in Sweden in 1430. Only once did Erik enter Norway, but it is on record that he on one occasion referred to Norwegians as 'an uncouth, bestial and savage people.'

On the death of King Christopher of Bayern in 1448 the 'Kalmar Union' temporarily dissolved, but Norway and Denmark were reunited under Christian I in 1450—a marriage of the two nations that endured till they were divorced in 1814. Christian I donated estates, castles and bishop's thrones to Danes and Germans contrary to his assurances, and so began the rule of foreign absentee landlords and feudal chieftains in North Norway. (It was, of course, Christian I who pawned the Orkneys and Shetlands to the King of the Scots.) In 1483 he was succeeded by King Hans as 'fully-empowered Lord over the Kingdom of Denmark and Norway,' after being compelled to grant immense privileges to the nobles and clergy. Sweden crowned King Hans in 1497, thereby restoring the 'Union of Kalmar.' Christian II was crowned in Oslo in 1514, but lost his throne to his uncle Frederik I in 1523.

The Reformation

King Christian II had acted as 'statholder' for several years before becoming King of Norway in 1513. He had secured the appointment of a Dane, Erik Valkendorf, as Archbishop of Trondheim in 1511. Valkendorf travelled up to Finnmark and earned considerable popularity, but, being suspected by Sigbrit of having had a hand in the death of Dyveke, he removed himself to Rome and died there in 1522.

The last archbishop in Roman Catholic days was *Olav Engelbriktson*, himself a Haalogalander having been born at Trondenes in the 1480's. He was elected in 1523 to fill the vacancy created by the death of Valkendorf, and received the pallium at Rome in 1524. In the ensuing twelve disturbed years he was the Norwegian leader *par excellence*, and the principal political figure in the country. His dual purpose was to uphold the Faith of Rome and preserve the independence of Norway. His chief opponent was Vincents Lunge, a Danish noble whose name lives on in 'Lungegaard,' etc., at Bergen. Lunge, who had married Margaret the daughter of the renowned 'Fru Inger til Austraat,' was 'statholder' in Bergen, and arrogated to himself autocratic powers between Lindesnes and the Russian frontier, whilst asserting that he had become 100 per cent Norwegian.

The Archbishop exercised considerable authority as President of the Council of State, but Vincents Lunge was ever ready to override the Council's decrees in the name of the King. Olav Engelbriktson saw that Norway's sole hope of salvation lay in becoming an independent kingdom and breaking all ties with Denmark. In this way began his collaboration with the exiled King Christian II that ended so tragically. The Lutheran King Christian III won the day and the Archbishop was compelled to flee the country in 1537, to die in the Netherlands a few months later.

It was Vincents Lunge who brought a preacher of the doctrines of Luther to Bergen in 1526. 'Fru Inger til Austraat,' who had many Haalogalanders in her service, converted them to the new teachings. Thus was Lutheranism spread through Haalogaland and Finnmark, the transition being effected without a blow being struck.

Finnmark from the Treaty of Novgorod (1326) *to the Reformation*

It has been stated earlier that, by opening markets all over Europe, the Hansa merchants in Bergen increased the demand for fish that laid the foundations of the 'Finnmark Fisheries' in about 1300. The first occasion on which 'settlers' in Finnmark are mentioned was in 1313, and in the pioneer days prior to the Black Death it seems probable that nothing more permanent than 'gammer' (turf-huts) were erected on frames of timber or whale-bone. These they would have taken down when they sailed south at the approach of winter. Kvens (Finlanders) and Karelians would have found the fixed settlements of north Haalogaland more profitable to plunder than the hard-living early settlers in Finnmark.

In 1385 Russians and Karelians broke the peace and raided North Norway, whilst in 1411 they repeated operations from Savolaks—'under orders from Novgorod.' In 1419, 500 Nor-wegians invaded Karelia, but the very next year the inhabitants of Finnmark and Haalogaland laid a complaint to King Erik of Pommern regarding murder and rape that the Russians and heathens had, and would continue to inflict upon them. This hostility between the Norwegians and their eastern neighbours continued for generations, even after Novgorod and its tributary lands had come under the rule of the Grand Prince at Moscow in 1478. Indeed the bitter memories of these murders was alive in Norway at the end of the seventeenth century, when Lilienskjold was shown the scenes of the engagements. The Karelians were generally the aggressors, and the union with Sweden aggravated matters since that country was frequently at loggerheads with Russia. The Karelians and Russians looked upon the Norwegian occupation of Finnmark as an unjustifiable entry into an ancient Karelian tributary land, in the same way that the Norwegians in the sixteenth and seventeenth centuries regarded the Russian occupation of the Kola Peninsula as an unwarrantable entry on Norwegian territory.

During these decades of strife North Norway was left to its own resources without any effectual aid from central govern-ment. The clashes with the Karelians were the tests whereby the colonists of Finnmark assured for themselves the perpetual occupation of the Far North.

In the fourteenth and fifteenth centuries the Russians collected taxes in the 'common districts' as far south as Malangen, and at the same time the Kvens and 'birkarler' (Swedish traders with the

Lapps, whose habitat was the northern end of the Gulf of Bothnia) arrived on the coast through the 'Finnish Wedge' (Skibottn). These latter taxed the Norwegian coast-Lapps all over the modern provinces of Finnmark and Troms and in the northern part of Nordland. The kings of the Union seem to have favoured the entry of the 'birkarler,' but when the Union was dissolved the 'birkarler' were forbidden to levy taxes on the coast-Lapps.

The 'Black Death' of 1349 would have caused a break in Finnmark's economy which, however, seems to have revived soon after, for in 1361 Bergen acquired the monopoly of trade with Finnmark, and its citizens travelled north taking families and servants with them to settle down there—many as agents of the Hansa merchants. But this Bergen concession did not remain a monopoly for more than a century, since after Christian I had confirmed the Hansa privileges he granted full trading rights to the citizens of Trondheim in 1455. The English also had unrestricted facilities to Finnmark trade between 1489 and 1524.

In the last two centuries of Roman Catholic times the coast of Finnmark became well populated by Norwegians who built several churches and chapels in the fishing villages. Some treasures of mediaeval ecclesiastical art have been preserved from the old churches at Loppa, Hasvik, Ingøy, Hammerfest, Kjelvik, Kjøllefjord and Vardø, and it is indicative of trade development that nearly all are of Hanseatic origin.

The Captain of Vardøhus and the Archbishop both owned fishery undertakings, and in 1511 Erik Valkendorf visited Finnmark and wrote: 'the country would not be habitable for Christians were it not that the catch of fish is so plentiful as to attract people to settle down there. And this fish, which they call "stokkfish," is so valuable and excellent that it is exported to nearly every Christian country.'

Tithe rentals in Finnmark commence in 1520, and at that date indicate a Norwegian population of 1,800 souls.

PART IV

FROM THE REFORMATION TO INTRODUCTION OF ABSOLUTE MONARCHY
(1536–1660)

NORWAY had to pay dearly for her unsuccessful revolt against Danish overlordship in 1535, and in 1536 King Christian III informed the Nobles and State Council of Denmark that: 'since the Kingdom of Norway had become so reduced in might and wealth as to be unable any longer to support a Lord and King, she should henceforth be and remain an adjunct of the Kingdom of Denmark and under the Crown of Denmark in perpetuity.'

Norway lost her State Council, and the King and Council of Denmark henceforth alone decided all Norwegian affairs. It did not, however, lose its independence entirely, being still intituled 'The Kingdom of Norway,' and the ancient laws remained valid. But as a rule it was Danes who were now appointed as its civil servants.

The defeat of Archbishop Olav Engelbriktson led to the fall of the Roman Catholic Church in Norway, and the introduction of the Lutheran Faith. The first Lutheran bishop in Norway was the Haalogalander *Gjeble Pederson*, who was born on Herøy in Helgeland in 1490. He became Bishop of Bergen, where he rendered invaluable service to the cause of education. The first Lutheran Supervisor of Trondheim was also a Haalogalander —Torbjørn Olavson Bratt—who was born at Andenes. He had lived for a while in Luther's own house at Wittenberg, and when a teacher at Copenhagen University had tutored the future king Christian III. He died at Trondheim in 1548.

The considerable properties of the Archbishop in North Norway fell to the Crown. These were in the main parcelled out amongst Danish nobles, but North Norway had too inclement a climate to have any strong attraction for the powerful families of the Danish nobility. When the vast holdings of the 'Giske-Bjarkøy' Norwegian nobility were split up, the new owners (such as Rosenkrantz and Rantzow) established no personal connection with their distant estates. They continued to live in the south or in Denmark. Some Danish families, however, settled in the North, and their fates were joined to that of North Norway through many generations.

Bjarkøy and Tjøtta lost their importance, their principal holdings being parcelled out. Large sections were incorporated in *Dønnes*, which is the only considerable estate in Nordland that has a continuous manorial history from saga-times till the twentieth century.

Meløy Estate, one of the largest in the North, belonged in the sixteenth century to the Danish family of *Benkestok*. That family remained in possession until 1661 and became celebrated throughout Nordland.

The family of *Schønnebøl* settled down at Bertnes in *Bodin*. *Inndyr*, in *Gildeskaal*, was granted 'noble' privileges during the 1600's, and had a short flowering period as the chief seat of Frantz Kaas. He was 'feudal lord' of Haalogaland, where he left an unpleasant reputation, dying in 1638.

With families of the type of Benkestok and Schønnebøl a new breed of landed proprietors and administrators came into being, who had no connection with trade and shipping as in saga-times. The service of the State became the recognized sphere for the nobility in the new order of Society and, after the Reformation, many of the seats that had been so rich in family traditions became official residences, some owned by the State whilst others passed as private property from one civil servant to another. Schønnebøls were appointed judges for many generations, and lived at *Steigen*.

That the great majority of administrative posts were given to Danes was a natural consequence of the Norwegian nobility having completely died out. By 1520 the five unmarried daughters of 'Fru Inger til Austraat' were the sole remaining representatives of the old order in the North.

In 1533 the Archbishop had no less than thirty-one agents in Nordland and seventeen in Finnmark, who collected his tithes and other perquisites. Comparison of these figures shows how rich the Finnmark fisheries must have been at that date. When the Reformation was introduced in 1536 these agents lost a considerable part of their incomes. Many of them, however, remained at their posts to collect what they could for their ecclesiastical masters after the Crown had usurped most of their rights. At the same time they began trading on their own accounts, and several swelled the ranks of a class known as 'knaper'—a name that is difficult to define. It was a Nordland middle-class, made up of schooner-skippers and retail traders, and from its ranks a minority of the Civil Servant class was recruited, who were of course native to the province. These 'knaper' carried on a so-called 'peasant-trade,' which the traders of Bergen and Trondheim considered poached upon their legitimate preserves and did their utmost to put a stop to. So the general public of Haalogaland addressed a prayer to the King, dated at Trondenes in 1571, begging for the recognition of the 'knaper.' His reply came a year later permitting the 'Nordlendinger' to carry on mutual trade in Haalogaland.

King Frederik II proclaimed the final defeat of the Hansa at the *Odense Recess* in 1560. His Lord-Lieutenant at Bergen from 1556–60 was the able and energetic Christoffer Valkendorf, who broke the power of the Hansa there, whilst it remained for his successor Erik Rosenkrantz to carry out the decisions of the Odense Recess. The Bergen Germans had the alternative of becoming Norwegian subjects or leaving the country, and thereafter the lucrative fish-trade of North Norway was free to all citizens of Bergen. Thus did the fishing industry of North Norway at long last obtain its freedom from the all-powerful Hanseatic merchants, who had themselves fixed the barter equivalents of the articles they bought from and sold to the fishermen.

The citizens of Bergen had acquired rights to Nordland trade in very early days, but they were not permitted to spend the winter months in Haalogaland. At the same time the citizens of Trondheim conducted a limited trade in the north, they mostly acting as middlemen for trade between Bergen and Haalogaland. Competition between these two cities often caused divided opinions as to their respective rights, and led to frequent disturbances.

In 1563 there were forty-four skippers sailing to Haalogaland, and judging from their names there were several Scots and Germans amongst the native captains. After the suppression of the Hansa in 1560 several English and Scottish merchants began direct and extensive trade with Bergen.

Haalogaland had its share of and interest in world trade, the market prices ruling in Europe for fish and fish oils playing a decisive role in the well-being of its people. The natives imported salt, iron, tobacco and alcohol, but above all corn. Rye was the staple cereal consumed, and this came mostly from Baltic countries. At the close of the sixteenth century price-levels changed considerably, those of Haalogaland products falling whilst those of its imports rose. This caused acute distress, and even famine, in Haalogaland through many decades. The beginning of the Thirty Years War was perhaps the most disastrous period, for in those years petitions for relief from taxation and conscription literally poured in to the King from Haalogaland. A drift of population took place from the fishing centres to the fjord valleys where cultivation of the soil might provide means of existence, and farming in Nordland then had its beginnings.

Recurring wars with Sweden also brought distress to the North, and in the last of these a newcomer from the South—*Preben von Ahnen*—played a not inconsiderable part. Of all the feudal lords of Haalogaland Preben von Ahnen is the first about whose character we can form some definite opinion. Though born on the island of Rügen and the son of a Pomeranian nobleman, he developed into a very good Norwegian. His first visit to Norway was to settle up an estate left by a relative, and he then appears to have become enamoured of the country. He acquired forests, farms and iron-smelting forges, becoming 'feudal lord' of Haalogaland in 1646. He continued to labour for the progress of the province and collected together a vast estate that stretched from Nord-Trøndelag to Finnmark. In the Swedish wars previous

to 1660 he was 'Commissioner-General' for North Norway, and
made an armed incursion into Sweden to destroy the silver mine
at Nasa (66½°). He constructed earthworks at Bodin, and for-
mulated proposals for improvement of agriculture in Nordland,
and for the erection of corn-silos. He also advocated granting
a charter for a market-town in Nordland, which did not
materialize for one hundred and fifty years.

When King Frederik III established absolute monarchy in
1660 he appointed Preben von Ahnen as his first Lord-Lieutenant
of Haalogaland.

SOVEREIGNTY QUESTIONS IN FINNMARK—1536–1660

The English in the White Sea

In 1524 the English lost their trading rights in Finnmark.
Somewhat later a scheme was hatched to find a passage through
'The North-East frostie seas' round the unexplored coasts of
northern Russia and Siberia. This attempt to find a north-east
passage to Cathay resulted in the discovery of the White Sea
route to Russia.

A company was floated that was at first called 'Merchant
Adventurers of England for the discovery of lands, territories,
isles, dominions and seignories unknown,' but this soon came
to be known as the Russia or Muscovy Company. Sir Hugh
Willoughby was chosen to be Captain-General of the first
expedition in 1553, with Richard Chancellor as chief pilot and
second in command. The three ships parted company in storm
and fog, two of them being driven far to the north. These two
vessels later reached the coast of Murmansk, where the crews—
numbering sixty-two—and their leader perished of hunger while
trying to winter in the Arctic wastes. The third ship, under the
command of Richard Chancellor, hugged the coast of Norway
and passed close under the *North Cape*, to which he gave its name.

Chancellor reached Vardøhus, beyond which 'all was unknown,' and found certain Scotsmen there who tried to dissuade
him from seeking the north-east passage. Chancellor waited a

week for the other two ships and then continued alone into the White Sea. He arrived at the mouth of the River Dvina and bartered some goods with the Russians at the Abbey of St. Nicholas. Thence he proceeded overland to the Czar Ivan the Terrible at Moscow, and from him received a general permit for all the English to sail to and trade with northern Russia.

The quest of the north-east passage was for the moment forgotten, and a second expedition to the White Sea was prepared in 1555 with Richard Chancellor in command, and with two agents appointed for the company in Russia and another at Vardø. This Russian trade flourished so exceedingly that the city of Archangel was founded in 1584 to deal with its flow.

This page of history cannot be closed without a reference to *Stephen Borough* who shares the honour of naming the North Cape with Richard Chancellor. On Borough's tomb in the church of Chatham in Kent can still be read: '. . . He in his lifetime discovered Moscovia, by the Northerne sea passage to St. Nicholas, in the yere 1553. . . . After his discoverie of Roosia, and ye Coastes thereto adioyninge—to wit, Lappia, Nova Zembla, and the Countrie of the Samoyeda, etc.: he frequented ye trade to St. Nicholas yearlie, as chief pilot for ye voyage. . . .' He died in 1584.

After the English had established themselves on the banks of the Dvina they began regular sailings round the Kola Peninsula. This constituted an inroad upon the 'eastern seas trade' of the Dano-Norwegian King, of which his Governor of Vardøhus enjoyed a monopoly. This illegal traffic by foreigners on 'the King's streams,' that is on waters regarded as being under Norwegian sovereignty, was a source of great annoyance to Copenhagen, and King Frederik II made representations to Queen Elizabeth of England that this prohibited traffic must cease forthwith. Emissaries from the two countries met in 1577, but no solution was arrived at since both parties maintained their rights. The King asserted his factual sovereignty by sending men-of-war north each summer to prevent fishing and trade by foreign subjects.

In their endeavours to compete with the English to discover

a route to China and India, the Dutch were also flouting the decrees of the King of Norway. William Barents is the most celebrated of these explorers, for he discovered Bear Island and Spitsbergen in 1596, and in the following year two boats from his vessels arrived in Lappland from Nova Zembla, where Barents perished. Skipper Elling Carlsen of Tromsø found his winter camp there in 1871, and brought the relics back to Tromsø and Amsterdam.

In 1583 England recognized the rights of the King of Norway to the waters of the Arctic Ocean, and the Muscovy Company paid one hundred rosenobles annually for the right to sail to the White Sea, in addition to a duty paid by each of their vessels calling at Vardøhus.

King Christian IV's Visit to Finnmark (1599)

Towards the close of the sixteenth century three kingdoms overlapped one another in the north, and King Christian decided to maintain his rights in those parts. All the territory between the Bay of Kola in the east and Tysfjord had been regarded as tributary to Norway from earliest times. This claim was never admitted by Russia and Sweden, whilst the medley of races there caused difficulties. The mountain-Lapps roamed around in the districts common to all three kingdoms, and when they moved down to the coast the tax-gatherers followed them and enforced their demands. Gradually the situation became so involved that those dwelling in Finnmark were taxed by all three Powers. At the Peace of Teusina in 1595 Russia transferred to Sweden all her rights in the territory between Malangen and Varanger, and so Sweden became Norway-Denmark's principal rival in those parts.

A Dutch map of the territory around the Arctic Ocean came into the hands of King Christian IV in 1597. To his indignation he noticed that an area which he regarded as being under his Norwegian sovereignty was labelled Swedish. Christian considered that a matter of great importance, and determined to assert Norway's rights in Finnmark. He appointed energetic officials as his lieutenants in the districts in question, and paid a visit there himself in 1599 to examine conditions personally and to show his country's flag.

On board his flagship *Victor* (with eight other ships in company), he insisted on being styled 'Captain Christian Frederiksen,' and anyone referring to him under any other title did so under pain of death. The squadron anchored at Vardø on May 14, 1599, when the King and his guests celebrated the event so bibulously that one of his captains, Alexander Durham, a Scottish mercenary, had a stroke and had to be carried ashore. Two vessels from Hull were arrested and their crews brought on board *Victor*. Incidentally it is stated in the account what a miserable place Vardø was, and that from the sea the church looked such a mean edifice that the cook mistook it for a reindeer! There was a frightful stench of fish—codheads and fishbones being exposed to dry all over the place.

Christian sailed on to a pretty harbour on the island of Kildin, and then to Oltin in Murmansk where two English ships were lying, whose crews were put in irons on board *Victor*. Here some Russians and Lapps came aboard, and after being treated to 'Alicante' wine they behaved like swine. The *Victor* then ran into foul weather, so the two English captains were taken out of irons, and it was they who saved the ship and took her in to Tiberi harbour, where they found about fifty Russian fishermen.

This seizure of English vessels by Christian led to tense relations with England, but these improved somewhat after the death of Queen Elizabeth in 1603. The use of the route past Vardøhus continued, and King Christian issued instructions as to Customs demands in 1609 that permitted English, Dutch and other foreign nations to have 'sea-passage on the King's streams' east of Vardøhus, with right to trade with Russians and Lapps there. It was, however, stipulated that they should run into Vardøhus for Customs clearance on their homeward voyage. By a special decree of 1608, however, the Dutch were forbidden to purchase fish.

The opening of the route to the White Sea by the English caused the question of sovereignty over the Lappmarks to become a matter of some importance, and then Russia for the first time effected a serious occupation of the Kola Peninsula.

As late as 1600 petitions from citizens of Bergen and Trondheim refer to the Kola Peninsula as Norwegian territory, but it appears that by that time the Russians regarded the ocean off Vardøhus to be theirs, since they tried to collect duty on fish caught by British and Dutch vessels. Russia, however, had no naval force to assert her claims.

The first Russian colonist on the north side of the Kola Peninsula seems to have been the hermit *Trifon*, a former pirate-chief. In 1524 he erected a hut on the Peisen River about four miles from the head of Peisenfjord, and later built a church on the spot. In 1556 Trifon visited Ivan the Terrible in Moscow, who granted lands to his monastery that included all the eastern part of Norwegian Sydvaranger as far as Neiden: 'all the coast and the land between the fjords, all islands, rivers and hills. . .' and rule over the Lapps within the territory mentioned. In this gift the Czar disposed of ancient Norwegian territory, and of *common districts* as though they were exclusively Russian.

In 1572 the monastery was carrying on fishing between the 'Fishermen's Peninsula' and the head of Varangerfjord, and was building boats on the Peisenfjord and the Pasvik River, as well as operating a considerable salt-extraction plant. They built several churches in the district—one at the estuary of the Peisen, one on the Pasvik River in honour of *Boris and Gleb* (consecrated 1565), and a chapel on the River Neiden. The monastery was destroyed by Kven raiders in 1589, it remained in ruins and never regained prosperity.

The Danish-Norwegian Government first took up the question of Russian encroachment in the 1560's, and in 1571 a Danish Embassy laid their case before Ivan the Terrible in Moscow, who replied that he would have the question examined on the spot and send an embassy with his answer. In 1573 Russian agents came to Lappland, where they fixed the frontier on the Pasvik River and removed all Russians from the Polmak. Thus was all the intervening land returned to Norway.

In 1582 King Frederik II sent a fleet to the Arctic asserting that 'Kola belongs to us just as much as it does to Russia.' The Czar retaliated with a bitter letter to Frederik: 'There stands on the Murman Sea within our patrimony a monastery named *Petsjenga*, opposite to the town of Vardø in your Norway. It has been there seventy years [*sic*] and we have had no protest concerning it.'

In 1584 Frederik II sent a ship to the Arctic, whose captain had a conference with the Abbot and his Counsellors in Peisenfjord. They sailed east and made demands in the name of their king, but reported that the Russian grip on the Murmansk Peninsula had become so secure that mere requests or protests would not succeed in regaining it for Norway.

In 1585 the new Czar declared that Lappland was within his patrimony, which included Petsjenga Abbey, Kola, Neiden and Pasvik. In a later exchange of letters the Czar asserted that historically 'also the town of Vardø is built within our patrimony —the Lappish Land.'

In 1595 Christian IV instructed his frontier commissioners that *all* Lappland had for many centuries belonged to the kings of Norway, as Saxo and Sebastian Munster had affirmed. Lappland stretched from Norway to Karelia, and the Russians themselves still employed the term 'Murmanska Sembla' (the Northmen's country).

In 1597 Christian IV sent ambassadors to Russia to demand immediate surrender of Petsjenga Monastery, and to obtain accurate information as to the extent of Russian Lappland. *Boris Godunov* ascended the throne while the embassy was at Moscow, and his reply was: 'the Lapp country is from ancient times a perpetual patrimony of the Czar's majesty, belonging to Great Novgorod with the Dvina country.' According to investigations made by Russian agents in Lappland the frontier of Norway is the River Skibottn, whose source is on the Swedish frontier, and falls into the sea fifty versts from the King's town of Tromsø, more than 1,000 versts from the Czar's fort of Kola. Behind this river the Russian tax collectors had collected taxes, and even the King's town of Vardø with its attached districts lay within the Czar's patrimony. Therefore King Christian ought to hand over this town to the Czar or let it be razed to the ground. Godunov, however, stated his willingness to send envoys to Kola to negotiate a frontier.

In the autumn of 1601 Christian sent a fresh embassy to Moscow. They were to assert the King's rights to the whole of Lappland and demand its return 'in continenti.' Petsjenga Monastery was to be handed over at latest June 9, 1602. The reply was a definite refusal on all points, and when the Danes demanded 50,000 thalers in compensation the Czar retorted that although he owned plenty of territory he would not give up one foot of Lappland. He declared that the correct frontier between Norway and Lappland was the Tana River, and the Russians would remain thereon. The only decision arrived at was that a meeting should be held on the frontier.

Godunov, however, wished to arrange a marriage between Christian's brother Hans and his daughter Aksinia, and the Danish Embassy were instructed to influence Aksinia to effect a division of Lappland, either on a parallel of latitude or along a meridian. But Prince Hans died, and so Godunov reverted to a frontier meeting. The Russians based their case on the ancient legend of the Karelian chieftain Vassiliev, who had conquered Lappland and made it tributary to Novgorod. Finally, the Czar agreed that the River Pasvik should form the frontier, the Church of Boris Gleb to be on the King's side, but he would retain the Monastery of Petsjenga.

The embassy brought back a letter from Boris Godunov dated February 11, 1603, in which he agreed to the above frontier, but Christian replied that all Lappland was his, and so Godunov's proposed frontier did not materialize. During all Christian IV's reign (he died 1648) he maintained his right to the whole of the Kola Peninsula—not only theoretically but as an actual political demand, which was repeated again and again during diplomatic negotiations with Russia, admittedly without result.

Sweden's ambitions in the sixteenth century were to incorporate the whole of Lappland and the mainland coast of Norwegian Finnmark (from Kandalaks to Tysfjord) in the realm of Sweden-Finland. In 1539 a Swedish map placed the 'Swedish Arms' near Murmansk, with the legend below: 'The Kingdom of Sweden extends as far as here.' This was the policy of Gustav Vasa.

In 1589 a Swedish-Finnish force had burnt the Russian monastery at Petsamo, but its attack on Kola failed. On May 18, 1595, the *Treaty of Teusina* was signed between Sweden (with Finland) and Russia. In this Treaty Sweden abandoned her extensive demands for sovereignty (and taxation rights) on the White Sea and Kola Peninsula. But Teusina was a great victory for Swedish policy in that the Nöteborg Treaty of 1323 was not mentioned, and still more because the ancient Swedish insistence on their rights to a section of the shores of the Arctic Ocean was now recognized by Russia in a treaty. The new Swedish frontier with Russia was defined as: 'through the centre of Enare Träsk . . . through Lappmarken and so to the northern ocean at a town Neiden, which lies midway between Varanger and Paszemi (Petsamo) Monastery in Russia. . . .' As recompense for the Swedish abandonment of claims east of this frontier the Russians agreed to surrender their taxation rights to the west of it to Sweden. As the territory on both sides of the new frontier was either 'Norwegian-Russian' or 'Norwegian-Swedish-Russian' *common districts*, it followed that the frontier settlement could not be valid without the ratification of the King of Norway—and such a ratification was never made.

In 1600 Boris Godunov refused to recognize the Treaty of Teusina, and indeed wrote to Christian IV in 1598 stating that the frontier between Norway and Russia was the Skibottn River. But Karl IX of Sweden nevertheless secured its ratification from the new Czar Vassiliev on the death of Boris Godunov. When Karl IX died in 1611 no decision had been reached regarding the northern frontier, and no delimitation took place. Gustav Adolf abandoned his father's Arctic pretensions, which had in the meantime been stultified by the Kalmar War and the Peace of Knäred in 1613. At the Peace of Stolbova in 1617 the difficult question of Finland's northern frontier was avoided, and so remained undelimited.

The Treaty of Teusina was, in fact if not in form, a threat to Norway's right to Finnmark, in that it gave Sweden grounds for claiming that she now possessed two-thirds of all its area as far south as Malangen. The Swedish king considered that Teusina established a partition of Finnmark between Russia and Sweden, and Karl IX worked to make this actual. He was foiled only by the firm attitude of Christian IV, who instructed his Governor of Vardøhus to prevent the Swedes collecting taxes in his province, whilst he himself was to collect taxes there—even from Russians.

Dano-Swedish Hostilities

In 1600 Danish and Swedish commissioners met at Kungsbäcka to interpret the extent of Swedish pretensions in Lappland, and to determine whether these covered only the inhabitants or land and coast as well. Karl's minimum claim was Varanger, Vadsø and Alten, his maximum being all the mainland to the north of Tysfjord—'where Norway's territory ends.'

The next meeting was held at Fläback in 1603, where the Swedes maintained that their Torne Lappmark extended from Tysfjord to Varanger and out to the Atlantic seaboard. Karl IX energetically proceeded to assert Swedish sovereignty over all Finnmark's mainland from Tysfjord to Varanger, and on June 16, 1604, ordered the posting of sheriffs along that coast to collect tax from all Norwegians who had settled at former Lapp settlements. He began to prospect for pearls, precious stones, etc., in the rivers and hills of Finnmark, and in 1606 issued his church-building programme, which included a Swedish church at Tysfjord where a Norwegian church had been built in 1601.

On September 8, 1607, Karl appointed a special *Statholder* in Lappmark (Norwegian Finnmark being included in this province), with orders to fortify Vadsø with a garrison of 100 men. At his coronation in 1607 he assumed the title of 'King of the Lapps in Nordland.'

In December 1609, Karl sent men overland to Alten where they were to build two ships and erect a fort for 100 men, and then they should proceed to Varanger and threaten the Governor of Vardøhus.

In 1608 Karl gave Gothenburg privilege to fish on the coasts of Finnmark from Tysfjord to Neiden—and in 1610 similar privileges to Lübeck and Hamburg.

It appeared for a time as though Karl's efforts would succeed, but the Lapps retaliated and the Norwegians forced the Swedes to abandon Vadsø in 1608. The coastal-Lapps in Finnmark were forbidden to pay tax to the Swedes under pain of death.

At a meeting of the State Council at Horsens (Jutland) in January 1609, Christian IV stated it was obvious that the Swedes intended to subjugate all Nordland and Finnmark, i.e. a considerable part of the Kingdom of Norway—their purpose being to maintain a fleet in the Atlantic. The State Council agreed that Denmark-Norway must be prepared to protect the rights of Norway's Crown—by force if necessary.

The Swedes then realized that they could not hold their own against the Norwegians in Finnmark, so Karl proposed a new frontier meeting which Christian refused. On December 11, 1610, the King of England was invited by the Swedes to arbitrate, and Christian thought the moment propitious to declare war on April 4, 1611. During the two years' war that followed the Swedes were driven from the coast of Finnmark, and by the time of the death of Karl IX on October 30, 1611, his aggressive Finnmark policy had suffered total defeat.

On November 29, 1612, the Peace of Knäred was signed, by which Gustav Adolf abandoned all Sweden's pretended rights —both sovereign and taxation—over the coastal-Lapps in the provinces of Nordland and Vardøhus. Both kingdoms retained their rights over the mountain-Lapps, but no frontier was determined between Norwegian and Swedish territory in Lappmark. That vexed question was not decided during the reign of

Christian IV, though he maintained his right to the whole of Kola Peninsula till his death.

In 1640 Olof Larsson Tresk compiled a memorandum entitled: 'The Mountain Ridge and correct frontier line between Sweden and Norway through all the Lappmarks.' This work, which was founded on thorough investigations carried out on behalf of the Swedish Government, names the frontier marks: 'from mountain to mountain with their names and circumstances in accordance with the opinions of such Lapps as have most knowledge of their ancient and immemorial rights.' It is of interest to note that the ancient frontier here defined is in the main identical with the present International Frontier that was delimited in 1751 after joint conferences and investigations.

SOCIAL AND ECONOMIC CONDITIONS IN FINNMARK (1536–1660)

An end came in 1560 to the control by the Hansa of commercial life at Bergen. Thereupon a common front was formed by all foreign and Norwegian merchants in Bergen to retain ancient privileges and to keep competitors out of the North Norway fish trade.

Fish prices, however, dropped disastrously for two main reasons:

(i) The adoption of the Reformed Faith in Germany had restricted the demand for fish during Lent and on Fridays.

(ii) The new fishing-grounds discovered around Newfoundland had given rise to a keen competition with Norway for the trade with Roman Catholic countries.

By the year 1600 the North Norway fishermen had to supply twice the quantity of fish for the same amount of corn as had been the case in 1530. Finnmark suffered more than any other district since it produced no corn within the province.

The Odense Recess determined that trade with Nordland and Finnmark should be conducted solely by the King's subjects. King Frederik II issued a decree on April 11, 1562, prohibiting foreign vessels from sailing north of Bergen, and compelling North Norway vessels to offer their exportable produce for sale in 'Bergen.' As early as 1569 these decrees had brought about a situation in Finnmark that obliged its inhabitants to send a deputation to the King at Copenhagen to lay complaints. This was the last occasion on which the Finnmark fishermen put up a fight, and in 1572 the Bergen merchants influenced the authorities to issue a decree that made it almost impossible for natives of Finnmark to continue to conduct their own trade. And in 1580 came yet another decree granting to all citizens of Bergen and Trondheim the monopoly of the trade with Nordland and Finnmark.

But these decrees failed to prevent foreign vessels from trading with Finnmark, and the produce of the North was bartered more or less openly by non-Norwegian vessels. A Dutch sea captain named *Jan Huyghen van Linschoten* made a voyage to these coasts in 1594–95, and has left a detailed account of life up there, together with a number of sketches of various fishing villages. Naval patrols were sent up from Denmark to arrest these interlopers, and *Alexander Durham*, a Scot in Danish service, was sent north in 1587 to put an end to this illegal traffic. Although he cruised around for a couple of months he never saw a foreign sail, but Bergen and Trondheim continued to complain of unlawful competition by foreign ships and those from other parts of Norway.

In the early 1600's the Dutch began to sail to the heads of fjords ostensibly after timber, but frequently to load fish. They had also leased the salmon rivers of Alta and Tana, but these were granted to Copenhagen in 1619. From that date Copenhagen began to be a powerful competitor to Bergen's privileges. Her ships were known under the general name of 'flensborger,' and they kept *East* Finnmark comparatively well supplied with corn and necessities on their voyages to the Russian Arctic ports farther east. Some of their skippers carved their names on a steep slope (between 1595 and 1616) on the island of Anikijeff at the eastern end of the Fishermen's Peninsula. One of these had visited that place six times in as many years, and he records that on his last voyage his ship was seized, but he does not state by whom.

In 1624 a 'flensborger' was granted leave to fish with six boats from 'Raftesiden,' i.e. Sydvaranger, where the inhabitants of Vardø and Vadsø collected firewood and 'rafters' for their house roofs.

For the people of *West* Finnmark, however, no relief came, they being left to the tender mercies of the Bergen merchants. When a series of years of bad fishing came between 1627–29, even those who had been well-to-do came to grief. Poverty stalked and Finnmark was on the brink of famine. The King had to step in with instructions: 'that any merchant who did not give credit to the public in times of need would not only lose his right to trade but all claim to outstanding debts.' In 1631–32 there was actual famine, and at an enquiry in Kjelvik Parish the question was put as to how many people had died of hunger. The priest replied that a number had died the previous winter, and when: 'he administered Christ's Body and Blood, they begged the priest for God's sake to send them food as they suffered great hunger, whilst that which he gave them could be of little use at the approach of death.'

Bad fishing years came again in the 1640's, and when the Lord-Lieutenant of Finnmark (Jørgen Friis between 1651 and 1661) received complaints from the Bergen merchants of the trade carried on by foreigners, he replied by pointing out the roguery in their own traffic with Finnmark. In some years the local authorities sent ships to Russia in the autumn to procure corn to cover winter needs.

There is mention of 'Frenchmen, Basques and several similar foreigners' fishing off Vardøhus in 1651, when King Frederik III issued a decree prohibiting this practice. It appears that the 'flensborger' had their best times around 1630, but it was not until 1657 that they 'abandoned their illegal trade in Finnmark.' The natives, however, only desired 'that such a time and such a trade might return to their land: then indeed it would be a great joy to be alive.' This was but a pious wish, since the 'good times' had passed away and, as it happened, at the same time as the establishment of 'Absolute Monarchy' in Denmark-Norway in 1660.

In 1589 there were seventeen churches and twelve priests in Finnmark, and an estimated population of 2,830 in 1597. In 1619 this was down to 2,650, and in 1679 to 2,070. Thus two-thirds only of the population remained as compared with that in 'the good times.' The 'bad times' really began in about 1600 and lasted nearly two hundred years.

PART V

FROM ABSOLUTE MONARCHY (1660) TO THE FRENCH REVOLUTION (1789)

HAALOGALAND FROM PREBEN VON AHNEN TO THE FRENCH REVOLUTION
1660–1789

IN 1664 the illegitimate son of King Frederik III—Ulrik Frederik Gyldenløve—was appointed 'Statholder' of Norway, and held that viceregal position until 1699. A policy of consideration for the needs of the Norwegian masses was followed throughout his Viceroyalty, much of the credit for which must be given to the great Griffenfeld whose advice Gyldenløve seems to have followed in his early days, though he later became Griffenfeld's bitter enemy.

In 1684 a decree was issued with the significant title: 'concerning the abolition of illegal demands.' This was the earliest attempt to put a limit on the number of liabilities that ancient custom had thrown on tenants in their relations to landlords. In 1687 *Christian V's Norwegian Law Book* was published and became valid. It was more or less a replica of Griffenfeld's *Danish Law* that had been promulgated four years earlier. It proclaimed equality before the Law, and was far in advance of most contemporary European legislation.

Griffenfeld spent eighteen of his twenty-two years in prison on Trondheim's island of Munkholmen, but his contribution to the freedom of individual Norwegians is still gratefully acknowledged.

The viceroyalty of Gyldenløve is looked upon as a bright patch in a long Danish overlordship that was at times far from being appreciated. In the World of Letters he is best remembered as the husband of one of his vicereines, Fru Marie Grubbe, whose

95

amazing life story has been immortalized by the famous Danish novelist J. P. Jacobsen.

Owners of the Soil of Haalogaland

Although in 1650 one-fourth part of Norway's soil was owned by the occupiers, the proportions were quite otherwise in North Norway where absentee landlords continued to be the rule. The Crown was the largest of these in 1660 when King Frederik III assumed absolute sovereignty.

Costly and disastrous wars had reduced national resources to a minimum when Denmark-Norway finally secured peace in 1660. The State was heavily in debt to several native and foreign capitalists, one of whom was *Joachim Jürgens*. He came from Itzehoe in Holstein, and had at one time acted as Controller of Crown Lands in Jutland. Later he was made a chamberlain to Christian IV who gave him his confidence. He was, however, an adventurer, and amassed wealth during the wars when acting as Contractor to the State, and by selling wines and jewellery to the Royal House.

Since the State had no other way of meeting its obligations, considerable Crown lands in Denmark and Norway were made over to him. By a deed of 1666 he acquired all the Crown lands in Haalogaland, which amounted to more than half the productive soil in the province. Even the establishment of the Lord-Lieutenant, Bodøgaard, and the residence of the judge at Steigen, came into his hands, together with every conceivable right and privilege over all properties transferred. And yet these North Norway lands only satisfied one-half of his claim against the State.

Jürgens, whose name was Norwegianized as Irgens, was then one of the largest landowners in the kingdom, but he also lived on a frantically extravagant scale. He resided mostly at Copenhagen where he owned a magnificent palace, as well as a country residence nearby. He possessed his own 'hotel' in Amsterdam, and acquired much property in Holland. In that country he was ennobled in 1674 under the title of 'Irgens von Westerwich,' and built himself an 'Italian Mansion' in a lonely and desolate spot.

5. Petter Dass—the poet of Nordland

When Irgens died in 1675 he was probably insolvent, and his widow, an Amsterdam lady, inherited a packet of troubles. The first creditor to cover himself was a flensborger—Lorentz Angell of Trondheim. In 1678 he took over all Irgens' holdings in Helgeland as well as his 'royal tithes' as far north as Vesteraalen. But the creditors quarrelled among themselves and with the widow Cornelia. An Englishman named Thomas Hammond, who had settled in Trondheim, acquired the ancient property of Inndyr in Salten in 1679. The legend that Hammond was a political refugee from the troubles of the House of Stuart is false, but his wife had the misfortune to give birth to a babe some weeks earlier than should have been possible gynaecologically, and so we know from a 'royal letter' of 1659 that he had to pay a fine to the Church for breach of its discipline. From this it seems certain that Hammond belonged to the higher social circles, and indeed his brother and daughter both married into the famous Angell family.

The State now stepped in with considerable claims on its own account. It appears that the original deed of transfer to Irgens had been ambiguously drafted. A Royal Commission having delved into that adventurer's dealings, found many of them to be fraudulent. The Crown then covered its demands by seizing the former properties of Irgens lying to the northward of Helgeland.

Irgens had a brother-in-law in Amsterdam, Baron de Petersen, who also advanced claims. This de Petersen had been a colleague of Irgens as chamberlain to the Danish king, and later settled down in Amsterdam and carried on a considerable trade with the East Indies. He procured the high-sounding title of 'Baron of the Holy Roman Empire,' etc. It seems he was most reluctant to take over any real property in Norway, and died shortly after he had done so. He had a son who was also a 'Baron,' and was 'Director for the southern and northern coasts of Africa,' and Chairman of an East India Company.

In 1728 the Dano-Norwegian exchequer was in such desperate straits following the Great Northern War that it offered to sell its rights in North Norway to the successors of Baron de

Petersen. They all declined to lay out any money, and stated that when their ancestor's outgoings had been recovered they would be satisfied. So the State put up their Crown lands for auction in the hope that the occupiers would bid, low reserves being put on. Even these, however, were too high for the occupiers, and so large landowners and capitalists acquired the freeholds. Among these was Anders Dass, priest at Alstahaug and son of the great poet.

It was not until 1751 that Baron de Petersen's estates in North Norway were sold in Amsterdam to a Trondheim citizen named Hvid, and so ended a strange story of absentee landlordism in remote North Norway.

Trade and Economics

An economic system had developed in Haalogaland based on the triangle of fisherman, merchant, landowner. Custom and legislation had established a necessary and satisfactory balance between these three. The fisherman contributed his labour—he had nothing else to give. The merchant provided the fisherman with the necessities of life and his stock in trade, and took the financial risk with his own capital and by obtaining credit from the fish exporter. The landowner gave to the fisherman the security of his home, with such absolute necessities of existence as a smallholding could provide.

This system worked well in practice, but the fisherman and peasant naturally came off worst. Life was not, however, made impossible for them, since if the merchant wanted to continue to trade he had every interest in keeping the fisherman alive. And this even in years of want, though the merchant might have to obtain credit to enable him to keep the fisherman alive. The law precluded the landowner from evicting his tenant except for flagrant misbehaviour, and so the fisherman felt secure in his home since any debts due to his merchant were not recoverable from his leased holding. The landowner also provided basic necessities in old age.

For many years the Bergen merchants had kept a stranglehold on every fisherman in the North through indebtedness, but towards the end of the seventeenth century this state of affairs altered considerably. It was now the turn of the citizens of Trondheim and the local 'knaper' to give credit and acquire the power that such brought with it. The change-over was regrettable, since the Bergen merchants had at least sent flour and corn north in exchange for the fish catch, whilst the local pedlars dealt mainly in spirits and 'flummery,' for which the women of the North have always been highly susceptible. Under a law of 1697 traders were officially appointed, and these operated in competition with the citizens of Bergen and Trondheim.

Corn prices had continued to rise until the 1650's, and were then stabilized on a level which, with few alterations, lasted 100 years. In the 1680's conditions were bad all over the North, with low prices for fish and poor catches. A series of petitions indicates growing poverty—North Norway becoming far worse off in comparison with the rest of Norway. The leanest years both on land and sea were the 1690's, and 1695 the most disastrous. Both the Lofoten and autumn fisheries failed, and there was little to send to Bergen that year. The corn crop was destroyed by snow and frost in August, whilst the storms of the winter that followed were so severe that fishermen could not put to sea. The Lieutenant of Nordland reported that as late as March 4th not a solitary fish had been caught, and that in one single parish there had been a death roll of 160 since the autumn.

In 1695 a capable Lieutenant of Nordland was appointed in Christoffer Heidemann, who at once set to work to reform conditions. Although he had been sheriff in Iceland he stated he had never seen such a low standard of living as in Nordland. Debts to Bergen merchants were the stumbling-block, and royal decrees in 1697 should have eased the situation if they had been carried out. But Bergen found means of evading, and Heidemann travelled to Copenhagen to make representations. There he died in 1704, worn out by his exertions for the people of Nordland.

As fishing became less and less attractive the population pioneered amongst the forests at the heads of fjords, and colonized considerable areas of productive land during the first half of the eighteenth century—especially in Troms bailiwick. It was therefore a catastrophe when three frost years occurred between 1740 and 1742. Those years of want formed the background for a report which the Magistrate of Tromsø district sent to the Chancellery 'concerning the tragic economic and moral conditions in Tromsø bailiwick.' This district lay on the limits of the trading area of Nordland, and also of possible corn production. The magistrate maintained that unless there were a change everybody in the North would be ruined. The debts to Bergen had risen so that many could no longer obtain credit, whilst the peasants were being bled white by the Trondheim pedlars and the 'knaper.'

After 1750 there are indications of a transformation in trade conditions in North Norway. Progress was made in defiance of opposition from Bergen and Trondheim, who held fast to their privileges, and considered that all the North was a part of their 'circumference.' A general desire for improvements in standards of living had begun to spread among educated people the world over, and the Government requested its lieutenants and others to put forward proposals for the welfare of the masses.

The main problem was now as ever the provision of corn and other necessities, instead of luxuries such as spirits and tobacco. The moral side of the spirit problem was always rubbing on the economic one. It was Hans Hagerup, Lord-Lieutenant in Nordland, who in his report to the King in 1752 had deplored: 'the crime of drunkenness—so bestial in the eyes of God and so deleterious for the welfare of mankind.' This failing had manifested itself in recent years more in Nordland than elsewhere, and Hagerup proposed that licences to maintain 'inns' should be granted in that province. Ten years later the first 'inn' was licensed at Kabelvaag in Lofoten, and thus was established a class of innkeepers, i.e. traders that lived amongst their customers and conducted import and export business over the immediate area that they served. This gave birth to a new aristocracy in North Norway who exercised locally a mild form of feudalism that was on the whole beneficial and efficient. A few survivors of these 'nessekonger' (coastal kings) are still functioning at some of their ancestral trading centres.

Petter Dass—Poet and Priest (1647–1707)

Scottish business men had for many centuries sailed to Norway to procure timber from her forests. Scottish manufactures and currency were bartered for Norwegian planks, and Scottish timber buyers married Norwegian girls. This mixture of blood enriched the culture of the native Norwegian stock.

In about 1630 a certain Scot became a citizen of Bergen. It is said that he fled from Scotland during the unrest of the Stuart period. His name was Petter Dundass—or Don Dass—and with him came a sister Maria who married a Bergen merchant.

Petter Dundass leased a trading-place in Helgeland—presumably Aakvik, on the southern tip of Dønna Island. Across the fjord lay the bailiff's house on North Herøy where the King's sysselman resided during saga-times. And in 1646 Petter married the bailiff's daughter Maren Falch, who was then 17 years of age. On her mother's side she descended from the noble family of Benkestok at Meløy.

Petter Dundass died a few years later and left Maren with five small children. She shortly after married the priest at Hadsel in Vesteraalen, and when he died in 1664 she returned to Helgeland and married as her third husband the Bailiff of Nord-Herøy, the home of her childhood. She entered widowhood for the third time, and even survived her son the great Petter, since death did not come for her till 1709 in her eightieth year.

Petter the priest-poet spent his childhood boarded out among relations until his aunt in Bergen sent him in 1660 to the Latin school there, where he studied for five years. And then in 1666 he passed on to the University of Copenhagen to study theology. Here he remained for two years before returning to Helgeland, as fully qualified in theology and the classics.

He had inherited the farm of Strand at Nesna, in the district of Rana, and here he settled down with his betrothed Margaret, a priest's daughter whom he was too poor to marry. In 1673 came Griffenfeld's gracious pardon for his breach of Church discipline, and permission for his ordination as chaplain.

At last the young couple were enabled to marry and become respectable in the eyes of the world. At twenty-six Petter Dass had attained his objective, but poverty nevertheless dogged their footsteps since the stipend of a chaplain was little more than nominal. They had, however, their small farm to provide most of life's necessities, and after seventeen years at Nesna, when Petter was 42, he was given the living of Alstahaug, the best in all Nordland. Alstahaug Parish stretched from Velfjord in the south to Lurøy in the north—from the ocean in the west to the frontier in the east.

In the old Rectory at Alstahaug—part of which still stands— Petter Dass wrote numberless verses that have lived through almost three centuries in folk memory, and are sung throughout Nordland, and indeed all Norway, till this day. It is the undertone of his deep affection for Nordland and its people that is the most precious gift of his writings. He sings as one who intimately knows and ecstatically rejoices in his subject, and his verse is remarkable for its interpretation of the majestic nature of Nordland, and revelation of the undaunted spirit of its people during a period of economic depression when poverty and near famine stalked the whole province. The most intricate religious problems of death and redemption are treated with as light a touch as is daily life in boats and fishermen's huts. All 'nordlendinger' understood him and memorized his readily assimilated rhymes. He became the venerated 'poet of the people,' and when the third centenary of his birth was celebrated in 1947, crowds flocked to Alstahaug in hundreds of boats from fishing villages in the remotest North.

His son Anders studied at Oxford before taking over his father's parish. He married the wealthy Rebecca Angell of Trondheim and became one of the largest landowners in Helgeland —a distinction that exposed him to much envy, and many an apparently unjustified accusation of avarice and oppression of the weak.

Hans Egede of Greenland (1686–1758)

Hans Egede was born at Harstad in 1686, his father being a resident magistrate on Senja Island, whilst his grandfather was a priest in Denmark. He began studies at Copenhagen University in 1704, and when only twenty-one was appointed chaplain at Vaagan in Lofoten. Here his troubles began when he refused to marry the widow of his predecessor in the living, and thereby defied ancient custom. His finances were of the slenderest, and life in Lofoten not too easy for so energetic a man. Having read reports on Greenland he was attracted by the idea of missionary work among the Eskimos, and of planting a colony on its bleak shores. So he gave up his living in 1718 and went to Bergen with wife and children where he persuaded some citizens to float a company to trade with Greenland.

His great work in bringing Christianity and culture to the Eskimos in Greenland lasted from 1721 to 1736, when he returned to Copenhagen with the body of his dead wife as tragic company. During those fifteen years he had been exposed to untold hardships, especially when an epidemic of smallpox carried off more than 2,000 souls.

Denmark then took up the work in Greenland and put Hans Egede in charge of a college for missionaries. Having been consecrated Bishop of Greenland he was later offered the bishopric of Trondheim, but refused.

He died in 1758, and is always referred to as 'The Apostle of Greenland.'

Gerhard Schøning—Historian (1722–80)

'The founder of Norwegian Historical Research' was born at Skottnes in Buksnes, Lofoten, in 1722. After a childhood at the school in Vaagan he entered the Cathedral School in Trondheim. Here he gained the nickname 'fatherland's man,' whilst at Copenhagen he was later known as 'the mighty Norwegian Patriot.'

He studied under Thomas von Westen (The Apostle of the Lapps) and Benjamin Dass, who was also a 'nordlending' and a near relative of Petter Dass. He became Rector of the Trondheim Cathedral School in 1751 and helped to found the 'Scientific Society' in 1760. From 1765 he occupied the chair of Old Norse at Sorø Academy in Denmark.

Schøning wrote numberless papers based on the ancient sagas, and propounded the theory that Norway had been first peopled by immigration from north of the Gulf of Bothnia. His great work—*The History of the Kingdom of Norway*—was begun in 1771, but only three volumes had been finished when he died in 1780.

Administrative Reforms

In 1787 the ancient appointment of 'Lagmann' (man-of-law or judge) of Haalogaland, who had resided at Steigen since its initiation in 1190, was abolished. And in the same year the bailiwicks of Senja and Tromsø were transferred from Nordland to the Province of Finnmark.

The age-old name of 'Haalogaland' fell into abeyance—to be revived in 1920 when the Bishop of Tromsø became 'Bishop of Haalogaland.'

FINNMARK FROM 1660 TO FREEDOM OF TRADE (1789)

Economic History

As the price of corn rose and that of fish fell conditions grew worse and worse in Finnmark. Here, on the outer bleak skerries, the dwellers in the fishing villages were less fortunate than those in neighbouring Nordland, and could not grow even an ear of corn for their own needs. They were entirely dependent on the goodwill of the buyers of their occasionally unwanted fish. This is the background of the State policy of 'Monopolies' that was started in Finnmark in 1681, and pursued almost continuously for one hundred years.

Even before the granting of this first *Monopoly* Bergen was master of Finnmark's trade, and it was on the representation of Bergen that the Government was induced to try the experiment of monopoly, for a period of six years.

104

Jurisdiction over Finnmark was also given to the city council of Bergen, and the office of Lord-Lieutenant of Finnmark abolished. This type of concession is unique in Norway, and can only be explained away by the consideration that Finnmark was a territory that had anciently been tributary to the King in person.

The Decree of 1681 led to an improvement in the first days. The principals in Bergen gave more generous credit, and in the main did their best to fulfil expectations. But the fishermen conceived the idea that the merchants were pledged to support them and to procure supplies. So the Bergen merchants again tightened up credit, whereupon the public and officials complained 'of the bad housekeeping that was being kept in Finnmark.'

The result was that in 1684 the King deprived Bergen Council of its authority, and again appointed a Lord-Lieutenant. This was *Lilienskiold*, an able man and a convinced opponent of the merchant's monopoly. In 1685 he was sent up to Finnmark in company with Bergen's Lord-Lieutenant: 'to bring order out of the distressing and confused conditions prevailing there.'

The chief complaint against the Decree of 1681 was the fact that Finnmark had been insufficiently provisioned. There were few charges against Bergen's administration since they had allowed everything to run along the former lines. The 'flensborgers' were asked if they desired the monopoly, but they had lost interest. Neither did the Trondheim merchants desire to take the risk now that times were bad. It was believed at one time that Glückstadt might take over, but in the end Bergen alone would accept the responsibility, since prospects of dividends were too slender.

This resulted in Finnmark's trade being handed over to a consortium in Bergen by a Royal Decree of 1687. The interests of the public were protected by a series of clauses, but the decree did not effect the anticipated improvement and there was soon 'such a wailing and complaint as has never been known in a Christian and peaceful country.' Officials in East Finnmark actually had to carry on trade themselves to prevent the public dying of starvation. Russian schooners from Kola brought corn and flour, although this traffic was prohibited by law. The Bergen merchants protested, and so Lilienskiold made the long journey to Copenhagen to ventilate the wrongs of the inhabitants of Finnmark.

The Government appointed a new Commission for Finnmark in 1690, which found that out of 800 families there, not less than 377 received no assured supplies of food. The officials were acquitted for their action in trading, and the 'octroi' of 1687 was cancelled. This Commission considered it essential to interest capital to invest in Finnmark, which was thereupon divided into seven trading areas that were offered to the highest bidders. The Bergen merchants were eager to bid, and six of them obtained the monopolies. They took over all former trading-places at value, and thereafter the survivors of the earlier independent trading community in Finnmark disappeared. But this proposed solution also led to loss and damage to all parties to it, and brought no improvements whatsoever. Very soon there remained only three Bergen merchants in active trade, who were supposed to provision all Finnmark. A sworn statement from Bergen in 1701 declared that several merchants there had been irretrievably ruined.

Yet another Commission was of the unanimous opinion that the trade monopoly should remain with Bergen, and a new 'octroi' was decreed in 1702, that twelve or sixteen of the most stable merchants in Bergen should form a trading company. But this new venture had no success, and when the 'octroi' period ran out in 1714 it was unable to collect considerable debts due in Finnmark. The reason given was: 'That the fisheries had failed to an astonishing degree for several years in succession.' But behind all the local difficulties lay the evils of two European wars—the War of the Spanish Succession and the Great Northern War.

Lilienskiold did not live to see what he and the public of Finnmark most desired, namely complete free trade. He died in 1703 and was buried in Holmens Church, Copenhagen. But during his last stay in the capital he had presented King

Frederik IV with his beautifully illustrated manuscript *Speculum Boreale*, which will for all time provide a tangible souvenir of the man and his work for Finnmark. It gives a reliable and detailed account of the glories of Finnmark's nature, of its products, ways of life of its inhabitants, their history and administration from ancient times to 1698. Lilienskiold portrays more clearly than any of his predecessors the tragic contrast between 'the good times' and conditions during monopoly.

By a Decree of 1715 there was to be free and unhindered trade for all citizens of Bergen and Trondheim as well as for 'nordlendinger.' Many circumstances led the Government to the experiment of free trade—prices for fish were rising, Russia was Norway's ally, but perhaps Lilienskiold's *Speculum Boreale* had exercised the greatest influence. All goods to and from Finnmark in Norwegian bottoms were to be free of customs duty, but foreign skippers were excluded under threat of loss of ship and cargo.

This period of free trade seems to have been blessed with comparatively good fishing seasons, and progress gave the people new courage and enterprise. But, directly the Great Northern War ended, a serious crisis in the level of fish prices occurred, which showed itself in full force after 1725. The cities in the South sent insufficient food to provide the bare necessities of life, and there was once again a shortage of fishing gear. Catches decreased and the people lost heart. In 1727 the citizens of Glückstadt applied for the monopoly of Finnmark trade, and Bergen sent in a similar petition. In 1728 the King decided that the trade should be leased to the highest bidders. These were said to be some citizens of Copenhagen, but there is some doubt whether the amount of the bid was the deciding factor since relations with Russia had worsened, and the Government may have desired to retain the trade of Finnmark in safe hands.

All through the eighteenth century Russian schooners entered the harbours, especially in Finnmark and North Troms, and traded with the public. They brought rye, and took away skins of marten, fox, etc. The Copenhagen Trading Company recognized this Russian trade after 1764 as being a necessity in the lean years.

Free Trade was at length introduced in 1787, to the indignation of Bergen and Trondheim. The Russians were thereafter prohibited from entering harbours other than those of the newly-founded market-town of Tromsø, Hammerfest and Vardø.

Social Life

An immigration of *Kvens* began during the first decades of the eighteenth century. Russian cruelties in Finland, and famine there caused by the war, drove these Kvens out of the Torneaa districts to find food on the Norwegian side of the mountains. It was particularly on the banks of the River Alta that they settled, they being experts in operating salmon rivers.

As to the way of life in Finnmark and morals of its people at this time, we have the writings of Thomas von Westen—the 'Apostle of the Lapps'—who had then just begun his work up north and was a zealous pietist. In a description of life there in 1717, he says that the characteristics of most of the Norwegian residents were 'sinfulness, ignorance, indifference, drunkenness, thieving and flouting God's Word.' But von Westen does admit that he 'has found some true Israelites at the end of the World.'

His chief complaint, however, was the inclination to indifference among the Norwegians. 'I have found on my travels more laziness among the majority than one could believe to be possible.' Worst of all were the youth, who had nothing to occupy their time. There were no schools, and idleness was the root of all evil. 'Women do virtually no work throughout the year. They spin not, neither do they weave. They do not row out to sea with their menfolk as the Lapp women do, and they keep no animals to care for.' He adds that the Lapps were disgusted at the laziness of the Norwegians.

These diatribes were written shortly after Free Trade was introduced, and he realized that much of the indifference among the people was due to lack of implements and other aids to labour, whilst the 'octroi' trade had given them an outlook without hope.

Von Westen deplored the fact that alcohol was permitted in Finnmark, as the tendency to drunkenness was on the increase. 'It is not looked upon as a sin by the inhabitants' and they: 'consider it a blessing and happiness that strong liquors can stultify their senses now and then'—but it must be remembered that von Westen was somewhat of a fanatic. What specially distressed him was that Norwegians treated the Lapps as inferior creatures and often addressed them as dogs.

The conversion of the Lapps in Finnmark was something more than an expression of religious enthusiasm, it was part of the State policy to retain the Province of Finnmark within the Kingdom of Norway. Thomas von Westen is one of the most remarkable personalities that the Norwegian Church has produced. He was a superb orator, energetic and fanatical, and was able to win over people to his way of thinking to a remarkable degree. It was just these qualities that enabled him to convert the Lapps to his teachings. He visited them in their tents and mastered their language perfectly. They had never encountered such a man, since all other Norwegians had shown disgust for them as inferior beings.

von Westen visited Finnmark in 1716, 1718 and 1722, and was instrumental in the erection of new churches and schools. He died in 1727, but his mission work went on, and a *Seminarium Lapponicum* was founded at Trondheim in 1752. This, however, failed in its purpose of training priests and teachers for work among the Lapps, and it was closed in 1774 as being ineffectual.

Travellers' Tales

We get a glimpse of Finnmark in the middle of the seventeenth century from the narratives of two foreigners.

In 1653 a French ship's doctor named La Martiniere published his journal under the title of *Nouveau Voyage du Nort.* He reached the Polar Circle in a calm, so they took a native on board to 'troll' some wind, and 'wind did come whenever the captain untied a knot.' He passed Vardø and came into Varanger Fjord, where he found Lapps who came on board and were disgusting. In each of their houses they kept a large black cat which they talked to, and would do nothing without telling the cat. The author, however, states that although it had the appearance of a cat it was actually a 'house-devil.'

Next we have the story of an Italian traveller, Francesco Negri, though he was more interested in natural history than in the people. Negri was an acquaintance of Norway's Chancellor Ove Bjelke, and came to Bergen from Copenhagen in October 1664. He later visited Ove Bjelke at Austraat, who gave him letters of recommendation for the journey farther north. Negri travelled as an ordinary passenger, and appears to have possessed amazing fortitude to put up with the climate and exertions on his way north along the coast. When he reached the North Cape, which he called the farthest limit of the world, he wrote: 'Now my thirst for knowledge is satisfied.'

In Finnmark Negri busied himself with animal and bird life, describing fishing and hunting on land and sea. He was most interested in the Lapps, and has much to say about their way of life, dwellings, etc. The Norwegians lived in turf huts, only priests and a few others who had means lived in timber houses which were transported from Bergen, as also was a certain amount of firewood. The forests of Finnmark had still not been exploited.

As for the wooden houses, Negri says they had windows with tiny leaded panes. The more prosperous had the wherewithal to eat porridge, smoke tobacco and drink beer and spirits. They were especially partial to the latter, and Negri kindly considered it quite natural that people who were exposed to such extremes of cold should consume quantities of fiery spirit.

The main livelihood of the people was fishing, and whether the fish was large or small it was sold to the dealer for a fixed sum, and he re-sold it to Bergen for twice that amount. In return the public demanded that the merchant provided sufficient flour and other necessary foods. The trader himself brought supplies to the huts and collected the fish, so that the people had little to do except fish, and to work at primitive handicraft.

Negri considered that people with such small outgoings ought to have been able to save money, indeed even to become prosperous. But there were few, especially among the Lapps, who thought like that. If extra money had been earned for fish they hastened to drink it up in spirits. There was luxury in some places, and certain persons owned beautiful silver such as spoons, spirit cups, etc. But this was more for the pleasure of possession and to give away as presents than to collect or use the articles.

The Norwegian-Swedish (Finnish) Frontier

The Treaty of Frederiksborg in 1720 put an end to the Great Northern War, and the English mediator—Lord Carteret—secured agreement that commissioners should be appointed by Sweden and Denmark to delimit their frontiers in Finnmark. But it was not until 1736 that steps were taken to implement this, and delays continued until final completion was secured in 1766.

Major Peter Schnitler made extensive investigations among the Lapps during the 1740's, and negotiations that brought about the final solution of this 'Finnmark Dispute' were carried on between surveyors and secretaries on both sides in Nordland during 1747–48. There were twenty-six points in dispute, which were finally narrowed down to the northern part of Nordland Province and the whole of West and East Finnmark. The Danes had the best of the negotiations since Russia was threatening war with Sweden, and so the frontier treaty was signed in 1751. The last of the frontier cairns was erected in 1766 at Golmisoivi Maddagietza, about twenty miles south-east of Polmak on the Tana River. Sweden (Finland) had to abandon its claims to Kautokeino and Karasjok, and the church at the former place was vacated by the Swedish priest.

Thus was the present international frontier delimited between Norway and what had been (previous to 1751) the Swedish-Norwegian 'common districts' in Finland's area of the Lappmarks. At Golmisoivi the Norwegian-Russian 'common-districts' were considered to begin, after the Treaty of Teusina in 1595 had confirmed to Sweden all Russia's taxation rights westwards from it.

After the death of Christian IV in 1648 all efforts on the part of the Danish kings to assert Norway's rights to Murmansk (or even to set a limit on Russia's further encroachment westwards) ceased for a long time. Each year the bailiff of Varanger made the so-called 'pretension to Malmis,' i.e. he journeyed to Kola to enquire of the Governor there whether he could collect taxes in Murmansk on behalf of his king. Each year he received the same reply, viz: that the Governor had received no instructions from Moscow. Therefore he could not permit him to do so, but that the matter would again be submitted to the Russian Government for consideration. This soon became a meaningless ceremony, which merely gave the Norwegian bailiff and the Russian governor an opportunity to enjoy an annual drinking-bout together. The 'pretension to Malmis' continued in this form right down to 1813.

The area of the Norwegian-Russian 'common districts' included most of the coastal land on the south side of Varanger Fjord—i.e. between Bugøfjord and the centre of the north coast of the 'Fishermen's Peninsula.' It stretched inland some thirty miles, and consisted of mountains, lakes, rivers, swamps and forests. Even in Schnitler's time, however, the land near the sea had been deforested, whilst inland there were considerable fir and birch woods.

The 'common Lapps' in Peisen, Pasvik and Neiden are referred to in Dano-Norwegian documents of the seventeenth and eighteenth centuries as 'Eastern Sea Lapps' or 'Russian Sea Lapps,' since not only were they under Russian jurisdiction but belonged to the Orthodox Church, and were therefore sharply divided from the Norwegian Varanger Lapps who also gained their livelihood on 'common district' soil.

It was not until the second half of the sixteenth century that Russian influence gained the upper hand in the Sydvaranger districts, and then it was acquired forcibly by the monastery. It is quite probable that the original inhabitants were replaced by imported Russian Lapps from the east, and indeed ancient sources hint at this. The so-called 'Skolte Lapps' in Sydvaranger

6. Stabbur (store-house) at Bossekop, from eighteenth century

7. Altengaard in 1799. The residence of the County Lieutenant of Finnmark

are anthropologically more Russians than Lapps. Their church at Boris Gleb (consecrated 1565) was the parish church for Pasvik and Neiden 'common Lapps,' and there was also a Russian chapel at Neiden that still stands.

When the Norwegian sheriff demanded tax from Sydvaranger Lapps he claimed this was because 'they utilized His Majesty's lands and seas.' The exercise of Russian authority in these districts was looked upon as an inroad into areas that had belonged to Norway from time immemorial. In early times the 'common Lapps' had desired to make the Bugøfjord a frontier—eastwards to be theirs and westwards to belong to the genuine Norwegian Varanger Lapps. These two groups were living in peace together in Schnitler's time, but by 1800 there was mutual ill-will and strife between them.

In 1694 the Norwegian bailiff reported that no Norwegian was living eastwards of Bugø, though previously some had dwelt as far east as Pasvik. He also stated that the Amtmand of Vardøhus had given Russians permission to fish in the Jakobselv, who had paid him two-thirds of their catch for the privilege, but that by 1694 they were making no payment. Incidentally this bailiff has left us an entertaining account of his journey to Kola in 1695 to make the 'Pretension to Malmis.'

In 1749 a small detachment of Russian soldiers came to Bugøfjord and asserted it belonged to the Empress of Russia. This visit had no result except to awaken the Dano-Norwegian Government to the advisability of ending the system of joint sovereignty, and that a frontier should be delimited to ensure Norway the whole or part of the Sydvaranger districts. But it was not until 1789 that a formal proposal was made to Russia, in which the King laid claim to the 'common districts' of Neiden, Pasvik and Peisen. If Russia would leave these districts to Norway, the King would abandon all other rights and pretensions. The Empress replied that she was not unwilling, but that at the moment she was too occupied with her Swedish and Turkish wars and suggested a postponement till they were ended. And thus matters continued until the dissolution of the Dano-Norwegian Union—indeed until 1826.

The operations of Russian fishing vessels spread gradually all along the coast of Finnmark, and representations were at length made to St. Petersburg in 1749. In 1769 the Czar ordered all his subjects to refrain from surreptitious trade and fishing in Norwegian territory. This decree, however, produced no effect, and the Finnmark Trading Company forbade the inhabitants to give lodging to Russian fishermen. So the latter brought timber with them from Archangel and built huts for themselves as far west as Sørøya off Hammerfest. In 1774 there were as many as 1,300 Russians fishing off Finnmark, and the Norwegians complained bitterly of their behaviour.

All the while there was a brisk trade with Russian skippers, and in 1790 the Finnmark authorities declared that their relations with them were 'good and blameless.' Indeed, Russian trade, as distinct from fishing, was always appreciated in Finnmark.

Changes in Administration

The seat of Government of Finnmark Province was transferred in the 1740's to Altengaard in Alta from Vardøhus fortress, which had become somewhat derelict.

Major Peter Schnitler, whose long labours concerning frontier problems have made his name memorable, was appointed Amtmand in 1750 but declined the post.

In 1787 the present Tromsø Province was united to Finnmark under the title of 'Finnmarks Amt.' The Governors lived on at Altengaard until about 1814 when they moved to Tromsø.

In 1866 Tromsø Amt was separated from Finnmarks Amt, each with its own Amtmand—the one for Finnmark residing at Hammerfest until 1888 when he transferred to Vadsø.

PART VI

DURING THE PERIODS OF FRENCH REVOLUTION AND NAPOLEON
1789–1814

Nordland from its Loss of Troms to Eidsvoll, 1787–1814

WHEN ancient Haalogaland was 'beneaded' in 1787 by the transfer of the bailiwicks of Senja and Tromsø to Finnmark, the Province of Nordland assumed the boundaries it still retains. The extreme North of Norway was then blessed with freedom in all its commercial life, whilst Nordland continued under the old order of privileged traders.

As early as 1775 peddling by the citizens of Trondheim was declared illegal. Those peddlars had pauperized the province by selling trash in a house-to-house trade. Henceforth their business could be carried on only at their depots—thus placing them in the same position as 'innkeepers'—whilst the public could deal with whom they preferred.

By a Treasury Decree in 1797 privileges were granted to schooner-skippers and other traders, and thus the innkeepers (most of whom owned schooners) supplanted both the old-style 'knaper' and the Trondheim citizens. The Government thereby created a privileged class of traders who were natives of Nordland and lived in it.

The objective was to ensure the better provisioning of Nordland, and a number of documents from the 1790's show that this was to some extent achieved. The supply of corn was the cardinal question, and during the war years (1807–14) the innkeepers played a creditable role in maintaining stocks. The trade in spirits was mainly a moral question, which, however, caused much agitation.

The 'good times' for the trading centres began in the 1790's, when profits were amassed owing to the neutrality of Denmark-Norway during the great European Wars. But difficult conditions ruled in the war years following 1807, when the twin kingdoms were dragged into the war on the side of Napoleon. The British blockade was quickly effective along the whole coast, and the 'lifeline' with Bergen was severed. After some seizures of schooners on their way north traffic almost ceased, and the situation in Nordland became desperate. To make matters worse crops and fishing failed over a series of years and many people as well as animals died of starvation. In Alstahaug parish alone thirty-two parishioners died of hunger in 1812 and bread made from the bark of fir and elm was considered good food. Within living memory a stretch of dead fir forest was still standing the trunks in which had been stripped of their bark about a century previously. The State did what it could, but action was taken too late.

In 1813 there was a currency crisis and banknotes were devalued so that debts could be cancelled at one-sixth of nominal. A good harvest helped, but a cruel winter followed and then a glorious summer blossomed in the year of independence—1814.

Bishop Krogh of Nordland

The history of Nordland during this troublous period centres largely round its outstanding figure Bishop Mathias Bonsach Krogh, whose interests and activities were all-embracing. He was born at Vadsø in 1754, and spent his childhood in Vesteraalen. In his youth he worked as a Lofoten fisherman and as a lumberjack in the Nordland forests. When on his way to Copenhagen to study theology in the autumn of 1774–75 his vessel was driven over to the Shetland Isles where he had to spend the winter— an illustration of the hazardous state of coastal communications.

Krogh became priest at Lenvik in 1781, later Archdeacon at Vaagan, and was consecrated in 1804 as the first 'Bishop of Nordland'—(the title 'Bishop of Tromsø' was first used in 1844). He was an enthusiast for decentralization, and as a 'nordlending' must have rejoiced at the creation of a diocese for North Norway and its separation from that of Trondheim.

In 1805 Krogh came to the Alstahaug of old Petter Dass as parish priest and bishop. Thus did he pour out his soul: 'Nordland is very dear to me. Here was I born and I still have to thank it for my livelihood. Therefore I want to give all that I am and have to promote its progress.' He knew the country and conditions of its people intimately, and having been shipwrecked three times could appreciate to the full the hazards of the calling of the majority of his flock. A brother bishop once remarked that he looked more like a sailor than a bishop.

It is enthralling to study the numerous phases through which Krogh passed. In youth came awakening and uncertainty, then a period of manual labour followed by a long fight for the advancement of his province and its people. In old age came a positive Christianity and an abiding peace.

He laboured to secure corn supplies through the war years, to found schools and lighten the lot of the poor. In 1808 he wrote to the Chancellery: 'Never has the condition of Nordland been more tragic than it is now.' He was a bitter critic of the 'innkeepers'—though he named several honourable exceptions. But he was no 'kill-joy' and gave high praise to the 'akvavit' distilled from potatoes on Tjøtta.

The use of coffee and tea among the wealthier classes in North Norway began early in the eighteenth century. During the prosperity of the 1790's the general public adopted the habit. Somewhat later Krogh wrote with obvious irritation of: 'the Nordland peasants' extravagance in drinking tea and coffee.'

Krogh might well be called the Father of Agriculture in Nordland in that he initiated the 'Parish Agricultural Societies' in 1811. In his prospectus of this Movement, which quickly spread over the whole province, he wrote: 'Agriculture is ever a more secure source of livelihood than fishing. The latter requires considerable annual expenditure, and the marketing of the catch is exposed to many hazards in this country. The profits are frequently forfeited entirely or greatly reduced, and the health of the fisherman breaks down earlier than that of the cultivator.

In the breast of the latter there will be found courage, determination and a healthy love of his fatherland, whilst fisherfolk are often weak characters and have little patriotism.'

The main objective of the Parish Societies was to drain potentially useful land, and the membership of each Society was very limited. They were superseded in the 1860's by 'Agricultural Societies,' on a less decentralized if more democratic basis.

Although Krogh believed that the future well-being of Nordland lay in agriculture, his first action after election to represent his province in the first Storting in 1815 was to bring order into the fisheries. He initiated the legislation that was enacted in 1816, by which limits of fishing-grounds for each parish were to be clearly defined. The owner of the fishing village to have inspection duties in his area, with sub-inspectors elected by the fishermen themselves, and many other desirable regulations.

This law admittedly gave the 'innkeeper' (*nessekongen*) great power and authority, but there was always the law above him and over every individual fisherman.. This enactment broke down many age-old customs and created new conditions both legal and proprietory. But under it the trading-places in Lofoten and Vesteraalen grew in size and prosperity during the generation in which this order of things prevailed. Both the law and the public accepted the patriarchial relationships that formed the basis for trading practices on the coast.

When Krogh was consecrated in 1804 he bought the farm of Belsvaag, which still stands nearby his parsonage at Alstahaug. On handing over his parochial duties in 1812 he moved to Belsvaag, which was the 'Bishop's Palace' till his death in 1828. His funeral at Alstahaug was the best-attended event in all Nordland since old Petter Dass had been laid to rest in the same church a century and a quarter previously.

Finnmark from the end of Trade Monopoly to Eidsvoll, 1789–1814

When 'Free Trade' was decreed in Finnmark in 1787, the Government also detached the bailiwicks of Senja and Tromsø from Nordland and united them to Finnmark. Its purpose was to give to the inhabitants of the extreme northern districts the opportunity of obtaining cereals from Russia under free trade. At the same time it was decreed that Charters be promulgated for the foundation of three 'towns,' since no town could come into existence in those times except by Royal Proclamation. Vardø, Hammerfest and Tromsø were selected, the latter in 1794 only after a severe dispute between the authorities of the two detached bailiwicks. The Lord-Lieutenant of Finnmark, however, continued to use the official residence of Altengaard in Alta until he transferred the seat of Finnmark's Government to Tromsø in 1814.

Trade in the new Finnmark was freer than in any other part of the kingdom. Traders and 'innkeepers' settled down wherever they wished, to traffic with the public, with Russians and Swedes, and to operate their schooners. They were also granted freedom from taxation for twenty years, and Finnmark began to flourish as never in the two previous centuries.

Efforts were made to induce capital to invest in Finnmark, and lists of dwellings, with inventories and stocks of goods in warehouses at trading centres in the province that had been the property of the Monopoly Company, were circulated among commercial circles in Denmark-Norway. Very few outside Finnmark, however, showed any desire to take over the fishing villages, the bidders being mainly former agents who had lived some time up north and knew local conditions.

Ole Sommerfeldt, who was Lord-Lieutenant at this time, had been a zealous advocate of reforms, and took a bright view of the future. He reported in 1789 (the first year of free trade) 'that the province already appears to have taken on new life and activity. If only the fisheries as a whole do not fail, which God forbid, and if Russia will soon make peace, there is every reason to prophecy a successful future for this province under free trade.'

It was most unfortunate that Russia was involved in the Swedish war of 1788–90, since that led to a cessation of Russian trade. In the late summer of 1790 Sommerfeldt wrote to the Treasury that so far Russian deliveries of corn and flour had been awaited in vain. Some vessels had left Archangel, but had been turned back by the Governor of Kola. But the war came to a close, and in 1791 the Russians traded once more with East Finnmark, whilst large schooners from Denmark, Bergen and Trondheim also arrived.

Under normal conditions Finnmark would have continued to progress, but retrogression set in when yet again the market prices for fish and corn fell and rose respectively, owing to the wars that the French Revolution had engendered. These had a damaging effect on shipping, and Sommerfeldt wrote that the war had 'induced the Danish and Norwegian shipowners to speculate in freights to France, and hence their interest in Finnmark trade had ceased.'

The state of public health in Finnmark was very bad at this period, and between 1792 and 1812 it was visited by a series of epidemics, to cope with which there was but one doctor in the whole province. In 1798 a raging epidemic broke out in Varanger, spread westwards and endured for years, being referred to as 'The Black Death.' A report in 1804 stated that two hundred and thirty people had died of it, and were buried in common graves in the churchyard of Talvik. In some places the dead had not yet been buried, and the Sheriff would have to send round twenty-four men in the spring for that express purpose. In 1805 another epidemic broke out in Langfjord—it was said to resemble jaundice.

Sommerfeldt retired in 1800, and in his description of Finnmark wrote: 'The high freight-rates of recent years have raised the prices of salt and other necessities to the detriment of Finnmark's economy. It cannot stand up to such adverse conditions during its growing pains. The lack of salutary competition, which speculators from Bergen and Holstein formerly created, is felt keenly. But despite these drawbacks free trade has already had a good effect on Finnmark. Instead of the neglect and indifference evidenced by the public, when they lived in wretched hovels and usually begged their provisions from the Government stores during the "octroi" period, the masses are now cheerful and industrious since they can only obtain credit through their own efforts.' Sommerfeldt also maintained that they were better clothed than previously, whilst in West Finnmark spinning, knitting and weaving as well as all kinds of home craft were being vigorously pursued. East Finnmark was lagging behind, but prizes were being offered there for spinning and weaving. In Alta, boat-building and tar-burning were being carried on.

In 1801 the Government sent Professor Rathke to Finnmark to report on its economy. On July 11th he visited Talvik, which he commends for its charming situation, good harbour and useful local trade. 'The freeing of trade has here as everywhere obviously had satisfactory consequences. The only matter for regret is the increased consumption of spirits and tobacco. The Russian trade is of the greatest benefit, and the standard of living among the masses is far higher in Finnmark than in Nordland. The reason for this is not the richer fisheries, but freer and more stable trade that allows the public to acquire flour and salt in barter for their own products.' He found the same activity in Bossekop: 'Enterprise and cheerfulness were at this time evident everywhere, in striking contrast to the hopelessness which unsatisfactory conditions of trade were causing this year in Nordland.'

Consul Buck in Hammerfest had been successful with catches off Spitsbergen and Jan Mayen, and free trade had trebled the export trade. Russian flour had come in in quantity, and actually been passed on to Nordland.

On August 6, 1801, Rathke arrived at Tana District, and learnt that the trader at Nesseby had begun to bake bread and brew beer for the Lapps, which they bought and consumed just as eagerly as spirits and tobacco previously. But elsewhere it was difficult to suppress those two commodities, which together with prunes, raisins, almonds and other 'edible tit-bits' were profitable and customary from days long gone by. The Lapps gambled at cards, with brandy as forfeit, so that they went home empty-handed and often with fresh debts. This was called 'to drink oneself tightly to the trader.'

In 1803 East Finnmark was in a bad way and many in Varanger had been near to starvation—had pawned their clothes, animals and fishing gear so that they were all but naked, and had no boats to put to sea with.

We get a glimpse of the life led by the 'innkeepers' in Finnmark at the turn of the century from the description of a visit to *Lyngseidet* in 1801 by two Swedish theologians who had crossed over the mountains. They paid a morning visit to the trader's house where they were courteously received and treated to liqueurs and coffee. The lady of the house insisted on taking them into her garden, which contained beds of vegetables, red currants and flowers which it was surprising to find so far north. Later they went to the church where the singing was appalling and the long hymns seemed never to end. After a plain but sufficient dinner of two courses their hostess insisted that the strangers carry out the local custom of kissing her on the lips— indeed all the men and women present kissed each other in this manner.

Conversation covered a wide field and the visitors were surprised to find newspapers and magazines from Copenhagen. But the service of coffee made the greatest impression. A quantity of utensils such as piled-up cups and plates, sugar bowls, tea and coffee canisters, tea-making machines, etc., were assembled near the door so that all could not fail to see them on entering. Coffee drinking was for the Norwegians such an essential habit that they would rather do without many necessities than abstain from coffee. When the coffee ritual was finished the party went out into the summerhouse to drink 'punsch.'

The Settlement of Maalselv

Serious floods in the valleys of Østlandet and Trøndelag in 1789 caused grievous distress to the farmers there, and several migrated northwards to the inland of Senja bailiwick at the instance of its sheriff, Jens Holmboe. The descendants of these early colonists are known as 'døler,' and still speak the dialects of the eastern valleys of Norway.

The valleys of Maalselv and Bardu are the real 'Kingdom of

the Døler' and, like their numerous secondary valleys, they differ from other valleys in North Norway. The Maalselv (river) is broad with a current that is usually gentle, and wide, flat, cultivable areas stretch from both its banks.

The mountains surrounding these flat lands are rich in forests, whilst at Malangsfossen there is a celebrated salmon trap, said to be the longest in the world. Potatoes and corn thrive well everywhere, red and black currants ripen, whilst cabbage, carrots, turnips and spinach are cultivated freely.

The first major Norwegian emigration to U.S.A. took place from this district in the 1860's, and in the next decade the 'American fever' robbed these valleys of many of their finest sons and daughters. In this twentieth century certain of their descendants pay visits to the ancestral homes, and the voice of 'the Middle West' can be heard across the gently flowing rivers through the light summer nights.

Louis Philippe in Finnmark, 1795

After Philippe Egalité had been guillotined, his son Louis Philippe found his way to Copenhagen in 1795. It is said he feared assassination, and so, with one solitary courtier as companion, he made his way up the coast of Norway, clothed as an ordinary traveller. They stayed at Bodø parsonage and then crossed to the Lofotens. The old guest room at Finneset, Kabelvaag, has ever been called 'Philippe's room,' and is still there.

They then moved on to Hamnvik on Ibestad, and a visitor can still have the honour of sleeping in the 'Louis-Philippe room,' and among the furniture that served him in his day. After a short stay in Sørsand on Bjarkøy, Louis Philippe reached Hammerfest in the latter part of August, where he was received by Consul Buck who was later presented with a gold medal in acknowledgement of his kindness.

The Prince was most anxious to visit the North Cape, so Consul Buck, having fitted them out with the necessary equipment, passed them on to his brother who was the trader at

Maasøy. They spent a night in a fisherman's hut near the North Cape, where he still maintained incognito being known as Herr Müller, whilst the Comte de Montjoie used the German equivalent of his name—'Frohberg.' It was possibly here that the legend originated of the mighty prince who came from a country far away in the south where the trees fruited apples of gold, but who hid his high rank under a simple coarse cloak. At first he was thought to be a foreign trader who had come to study the fisheries—a natural enough conclusion since he was forthright in manner and his requirements were simple. But his high birth soon betrayed itself, since his companion never addressed him without taking off his hat and lying on the floor at night whilst the Prince slept in the bed. They had spent a night in a fisherman's hut, and when the housewife went in to them in the morning she saw that the Prince wore elaborate uniform under his utility overcoat, and was smothered with crosses and stars in diamonds!

There is another story of an old woman named Brita to whom Louis gave a coin. She took his hand, and having read it said: 'People in this country believe you to be one of those travellers who pass this way now and again. But I know that you are greater than the Lord-Lieutenant, indeed higher than the Bishop of Trondheim. I know that you are a Prince, and you will discover that old Brita does not lie, for one day you will be a king.' Old Brita had indeed prophesied correctly.

Louis Philippe was one of the first tourists to visit the North Cape, and then he returned to Alta where he paid a visit to the mountain-Lapps in their tents. From Alta they travelled by Lapp-sledge across Finnmarksvidda to Swedish Lappland and spent a while at Muoniniska, then the most northerly Swedish mission station. They stayed with the Swedish priest, Kolström, when the Prince seduced the sister of Mrs. Kolström. A son was born, but by that time the Prince was far far away. So the lad grew up in the parsonage and took the name of Kolström. His descendants migrated to Norwegian territory on the Tana, where the Bourbon blood still flows in their veins on the banks of that mighty salmon river.

It was not until after Louis had left Finnmark that his hosts discovered his identity, but when he became King of France he did not forget his friends in the north. Forty-three years later —in 1838—he sent the corvette *Recherche* up to Maasøy with a bronze bust of himself, almost twice life size. But Maasøy's inhabitants had meanwhile moved to Havøysund, and there the bust was presented—to remain until the Germans burnt down the entire fishing village in 1944. It was recovered from the devastation in a badly damaged condition, and is now in Tromsø Museum.

When the celebrated Nordland artist Peder Balke lived in Paris in 1846–47, Louis Philippe commissioned him to execute more than thirty works, including one of the North Cape in which the King and his companion should figure in the landscape.

Four years after Louis' visit two other foreigners arrived in Finnmark—an Italian, Joseph Acerbi, and a Swede, Anders Skjøldebrand. Acerbi writes that their Finnmark hosts must have believed they were two princes in disguise from the fuss they made of them. These two men had come across the Swedish mountains and down the Alta River, whence they sailed for the North Cape. They were impressed at the way all doors were left open at nights and at the peace and security of life on the edge of the world.

Another war-time traveller was the German, Leopold von Buch. He arrived at Alta in 1807, having travelled up with the Lord-Lieutenant of Finnmark, with whom he stayed for a while at Altengaard. It was a remarkably warm summer that year, and Buch gives an enthusiastic account of the landscape and luxuriant vegetation. He had much to say about the Kvens, who made up two-thirds of the population of Alta. Buch then passed on to Hammerfest where he found the Russian traders a real blessing for Finnmark. He visited the pastor at Maasøy, and failed to comprehend how an educated man could possibly spend his life in "so grey a spot which is scarcely habitable even for fishermen and Russians." At Kvalsund he stayed with the trader, whom he praises highly, remarking that if the pastor has the souls of his parishioners in his keeping, it is the 'innkeeper' who has their material welfare in his hands. Lapps as well as Norwegians neglect everything in the world provided they can consume neat spirit at the 'trader's.' Hence unscrupulous innkeepers can easily be a terror to the countryside.

England and Norway at War, 1807–14

The outbreak of war found North Norway entirely unprepared. Vardøhus was the only existing fortress and no other land defences had been improvised. There was a scramble to form a Coastal Defence Force and Citizens' Militia, but no muskets were available except for a few so-called 'Lapp-guns,' such as were employed when hunting whales, etc. By the close of 1808 the strength of the defending forces was about 4,500, most of whom were recruited from the trading community, many being of little value.

It was not until 1810 that a Captain of Royal Engineers was sent north to erect defences at Hammerfest and Bodø. Tromsø was not selected for fortification since it lay so far from the open ocean and the narrow approaches were its best protection.

News of the outbreak of war reached Tromsø on September 11, 1807. It was clear that a blockade of northern coasts could be expected since North Norway would now be compelled to import necessities from Russia, that had become Napoleon's ally following the Peace of Tilsit in 1807. Rupture with England also meant that war with Sweden followed.

The capture of two north-bound schooners put fear into the coastal sailors, and not a single vessel brought food from the south all that year. So the Government bought 25,000 tons of corn in Archangel and it became a matter of life and death that such blockade as the British had established should be run successfully in order to import this corn. From August and all through the winter things went well, but 1809 produced immense difficulties.

On June 21, 1809, a British warship of forty guns passed Vardø from Kola and anchored at Havningberg, and during the whole

126

summer three English brigs—*Snake, Nightingale and Fancy*—kept a close watch on the coast. Many Courts of Enquiry were held at Bossekop to gain facts about the loss of Norwegian vessels.

Between July 4th and 9th the *Snake* lay at Hasvik on Senja, and Norwegian reports give an unpleasant account of the plunder and general behaviour of its crew, though there is some doubt whether a couple of local 'quislings' were not the actual malefactors. At Kjøllefjord vicarage, where Russian fishermen ransacked the house, the guilt was also attributed to the British.

On July 9th the *Snake* and *Fancy* bombarded Hammerfest, which was then a 'town' only in name, but had a few light guns mounted that were manned by local traders. A spirited resistance was, however, put up and both British ships were hit by Norwegian shells, but the result was a foregone conclusion. The account once again mentions theft, plunder and destruction, including the church. Wild excesses are reported and the inhabitants fled, whilst the two vessels lay in the harbour for a whole week.

The British blockade in 1809 was sufficiently effective to cause the natives to abandon their most exposed trading centres, and all Russian traffic ceased.

In 1810 the Norwegians fitted out a 'Finnmark Squadron' which kept privateers at bay whilst it cruised off the northern coasts. But it sailed south from Hammerfest on August 13th, and once again Russian trade became a dangerous hazard. On August 23rd a schooner was captured at Kjelvik by two English ships, and two Norwegians were held on board to help to work the prize to England. Bad weather drove her back to Finnmark, and the prize crew from the British frigate *Nymph* was brought in to Bossekop and thence forwarded to Trondheim as prisoners.

During 1811 the coast was left fairly clear and the Russians came early with their corn vessels—for the 'Finnmark Squadron' then had eight ships on station. A couple of its smaller vessels were chased in to Porsanger by a British brig during the summer. But 1811 was a bad year for the Norwegian personnel owing to epidemics which caused a heavy death roll.

In 1812 the 'Finnmark Squadron' was fitted out for the third time and patrolled the coasts. On August 1st a cutter sighted a large ship which had sent boats ashore for fresh water, but had hoisted sail again and was standing out to sea. The Norwegians believed this to be a merchantman and recklessly gave chase. For it proved to be the British frigate *Horatio* of fifty guns, under the command of Lord George Stuart, which had been detached from the main fleet for reconnaissance up to the North Cape.

Lord George anchored off Risøy and lowered a pinnace and three cutters to bring the Norwegian vessel to action among the narrow channels. In his report he wrote: 'I made a point of destroying hostile craft since they have inflicted considerable damage on our trade on this route.' The Norwegian cutter made the better speed and arrived at Tromsø early on Sunday, August 2nd, but the Danish commander there, Lieutenant Hans Carl Bodenhoff, did not expect further action by the British since they would have difficulty in negotiating the narrow waters. But they had picked up a trader at Tronjord who knew a little English, and forced him to act as pilot.

Lieutenant Hawkins, who was in charge of the four English boats, put men ashore from one of his craft and attacked the armed Norwegian vessels, one at a time, with the other three. The fighting went on with varying success, and at the third attempt on Bodenhoff's ship he killed Lieutenant Snyder with his own hands and repelled the attack. Entry was effected during the fourth attack when Bodenhoff was wounded first in the right hand, his thumb being almost severed. Later he received a sword cut on his head which made him see red. He sprang into the ranks of the British, killing two sailors and wounding a giant of a negro. After two more wounds he fell unconscious to the deck when the wounded negro, frantic with pain, put his foot on Bodenhoff preparatory to finishing him off. Lieutenant Hawkins threw himself between them at the last moment and thus saved Bodenhoff's life. Surrender followed the incapacity of the Norwegian leader.

8. The French Corvette *Recherche*, that took the bust of Louis Philippe to Finnmark in 1838

9. Finneset near Kabelvaag, with 'Louis Philippe's room' on left

The boats' crews of the *Horatio* apparently manhandled the Norwegians somewhat fiercely owing to the fact that all the British officers were more or less severely wounded and could not exercise control, whilst Lieutenant Snyder and the surgeon and ten ratings had been killed. The loss of the surgeon was a misfortune for the numerous wounded of both nations as a considerable delay occurred in returning to the *Horatio*, owing to the high proportion of wounded English and the fatigue of the remainder.

Lieutenant Hawkins handed over Bodenhoff's sword to Lord Stuart, who at once went up to the wounded Bodenhoff saying: 'Allow me to return your sword. You have made such good use of it that it would be a shame if you could not always bear it.' Then Bodenhoff was carried to the dead Lieutenant Snyder's cabin and the ship's doctor dressed his wounds before those of all the others, even the British officers.

Lord Stuart's report stated: 'After the most sanguinary action the enemy vessels were captured, but following a most gallant defence. . . . Our losses must be attributed to the desperate resistance which the Danish commander made, and to the more favourable position of his vessels.' In a later report he stated he would never have attempted an attack with boats on Tromsø if he could have foreseen how dearly victory was to be bought.

With so many of his officers wounded the captain decided to sail home at once, and reached Yarmouth on August 13, 1812. Bodenhoff had been operated upon several times during the voyage and lay for three months in hospital. In his report on September 12th he states that only the skill of the surgeon had saved his left arm, which had received a bayonet thrust.

When he was discharged from hospital he was sent to Reading, where all Dano-Norwegian officers who gave parole were congregated during the Napoleonic wars. There he met a young girl, Miss S. Cooper, who became his wife in 1814. He returned to Denmark after the war as a 'Knight of Dannebrog,' and lived partly in Denmark and partly in England when not actually at sea. He rose to the rank of post-captain, and was christened 'The Lion of Tromsø' by the public of his native land.

The unpreparedness of the Norwegian armed forces for the surprise attack on Tromsø harbour, led to bitter recrimination among its three sections, viz. The Navy, Coast Defence Force and Citizens Militia. They all shared guilt in having been too confident that no sufficient enemy forces could overcome the pilotage difficulties in the narrow approaches.

The 'Battle of Tromsø' was the very last occasion on which the armed forces of Norway and Britain fought as enemies, and the last two years of the Napoleonic Wars gave rise to no major hostile incident.

An American privateer, searching for British vessels, ran into Hammerfest for water in 1813, and on June 23rd of that year a Norwegian ship was seized off Nordkyn by an English frigate.

Peace and Independence Come

In 1813 the Danish Prince Christian Frederik arrived in Norway as 'Statholder.' After the Battle of Leipzig, Bernadotte (Karl Johan) Crown Prince of Sweden, hastened to attack Denmark, and dictated peace terms in January 1814 at the Treaty of Kiel, by which Denmark's rights in Norway passed to the King of Sweden.

Norway was united in its opposition to the Peace of Kiel, and was prepared to fight to the last man for independence, under the leadership of Prince Christian Frederik. He called a meeting of the nation's leading men on February 16, 1814, which took the decision to call a National Assembly at Eidsvoll to draw up a Constitution.

On February 19th Christian Frederik despatched instructions to all bishops and Lords-Lieutenant as to the procedure of taking the oath of loyalty, and of electing representatives for counties and towns. Not until April 14th did this notice arrive at Alten-gaard, though the Assembly had met on April 10th at Eidsvoll. Even in the town of Tromsø the election (held in the church) did not take place till May 30th, and so, owing to its remoteness, not a single representative from North Norway was present on April 10th or May 17th.

On August 14, 1814, Karl Johan repudiated many provisions of the Treaty of Kiel, and confirmed the Constitution of May 17th.

An Extraordinary Storting assembled in Christiania in October to approve the Personal Union of Norway with the Crown of Sweden. But yet again no representatives from Nordland or Finnmark arrived in time to take part in its proceedings.

PART VII

THE PROVINCE OF NORDLAND IN THE NINETEENTH CENTURY
1814–1905

Communications

MENTION has already been made of the inability, due to slowness of communications, for representatives to arrive at Eidsvoll in time for the adoption of the 'Constitution' on May 17, 1814.

The 'mountain-post' had ceased to operate during the war and did not reopen till 1822, and by it Stockholm papers were *only* four weeks old when they reached Tromsø. The 'sea-post' was much slower, and wind and weather often defeated the faithful postal servants.

There is a record of a round trip made in 1828 by a man who left Tromsø on February 10th by boat to Skibottn, and then by reindeer sledge to Karesuando in Sweden and so to Haparanda. From there by horse sledge along the coast of the Gulf of Bothnia to Gävle, and so to Uppsala and Stockholm. Thence to Kristiania via Örebro and Kongsvinger. On the return journey he drove to Trondheim via Røros and took the first opportunity by boat to Tromsø, where he arrived after continuous travel on June 27th, i.e. four and a half months for the return journey Tromsø–Kristiania.

With such a background the first steamer to coast in North Norway created a revolution, and became a mighty factor in its development. This vessel, the *Prinds Gustav*, was built in London, had a length of 124 feet, and was operated by the State. She took a whole week from Trondheim to Tromsø and nine days to Hammerfest, and created a startling impression on 'nordlendinger,' many thinking it must be witchcraft that spat out fire and smoke and could push its way against sea and current. They also believed that the noise of the paddle-wheels, and soot and ash thrown overboard, would frighten away the fish. Many protests were sent to the Amtmenn on that score.

This steamer service rapidly became popular with travellers, and certain foreigners have left descriptions of their experiences in its early days. Frederick Metcalfe thus describes the call at Grøtøy in 1855:

'At Grøtøy the steamer threads a narrow passage, so narrow that a biscuit might be pitched ashore. On the edge of this dreary defile lives one of the principal merchants of these parts. A boat put off from his house, full of gaily-dressed ladies, armed with parasols to keep off the intense rays of the Arctic sun. This large party is professedly escorting on board a single female acquaintance who is going northward with us.' This, however, was only an excuse since 'the dear creatures come to see and be seen. For many miles around there is not a neighbour who can appreciate their charms and attractive bonnets. They scarcely see a stranger except on Sundays and when the steamer calls.' He noticed two young girls carrying on a conversation from their boat, whilst they all the time primmed their hair and scarves with not a little coquetry. . . . 'And who can deny that those five minutes do not sometimes lay the foundations for future happiness? . . .'

In 1865 two shipping companies at Trondheim and Bergen took over the coastal service to the North, and at the same time local steamship companies were formed to service the fjords and outlying islands.

The opening of the Express Coastal Route (Hurtigruten) in 1893 brought North Norway several days nearer the remainder of the country, and resulted in the most spectacular development in the cultural and economic life of ancient Haalogaland. Hitherto six to seven days were required for the journey Trondheim-Hammerfest, now this was reduced to two and a half days. 'Hurtigruten' has remained, since its opening in 1893, the main artery in the life of North Norway.

All traffic was by sea, and such roads as existed were solely to keep up communication with the nearest steamer quay. The nineteenth century closed before the advent of the internal combustion engine required that North Norway roads should be more than dirt tracks.

The grand old man of northern land communications was Ole Tobias Olsen. A teacher on Hadsel Island in his early life, he visited the London Exhibition in 1862, and there noticed railway trucks from Scotland laden with fresh fish. With the idea of rapid transport of Lofoten fish to the markets of Europe he started his fifty years' campaign for a railway to North Norway coastal ports. He lived to know of the Storting's resolution of 1923 for the building of a railway to Bodø, and died the following year at the age of ninety-four. He had realized his life's ambition, though it was not until 1940—and then under the shadow of German occupation—that the first train steamed across the southern limits of Nordland Province.

Fairs and Markets in Nordland

'Fairs' provided an annual holiday for the dwellers in the remote fjords and outlying islands. These lonely people rowed long distances to dispose of their products and handicraft at the 'fairs,' and also for one occasion each year to consort with fellow-creatures who were not their immediate neighbours.

When 'innkeepers' were recognized by the Government many of them were privileged to trade at the 'fairs' on payment of a special tax. There were several fairs in Nordland, but it was the established custom at these annual events that dealings should be direct without middlemen, and thus many other dealers were present though the 'innkeeper' had the sole right to sell spirits.

The main fair for south Helgeland was at Tilrem just north of Brønnøy, which was a good centre for all the fjords and islands around. A Swedish traveller visited Tilrem fair in 1816 and wrote: 'We entered a deep fjord where many boats lay. The fairground lay along the beach where several timber booths had been put up. A number of dealers from Trondheim and Bergen brought their goods, consisting of bar-iron, bottles of perfume, tobacco, gloves, etc., etc.'

That short description applies to most of the 'fairs,' the most important of which was at Bjørn on Dønna, opposite modern Sandnessjøen. The week before the fair, things began to liven

134

up at Bjørn. Boats from the islands arrived laden with fresh, dried and salted fish, eiderdown and feathers. From the inner fjords came the fjord dwellers with convoys of newly-built boats in tow, which were loaded with all sorts of joinery and woodwork. In the harbour lay vessels belonging to citizens of Trondheim and traders from elsewhere, and from them barrels and cases were run ashore to the booths. Some booths were owned by the traders and landowners, and others by the peasants of the district.

When the 'fair Sunday' approached numbers of people rowed in from fjord and strait. The men rowed till sweat poured from them whilst the women played and sang. Some of the boats were run ashore and turned upside down to provide shelters, where the visitors slept for so long as the fair lasted. Food booths and coffee stalls were put up, and people sat at the long tables eating a variety of delicacies—one especial favourite being seabirds eggs hard-boiled—and drinking coffee.

There were crowds around the stalls, whilst down by the shore fishermen sold their catch, especially herrings, to the inshore dwellers. The fjord people had their booths farther up the slopes, displaying all kinds of joinery and woodwork that were in demand for the inhabitants of the islands. Dealers in manufactured articles pitched their tents highest up, and bundles of readymade clothes, etc., lay spread out on tables. Some Swedes came over the mountains and did a good business in ironmongery of all kinds.

On 'fair Monday' trade was in full swing and folk crowded the lanes between booths and tents. Quacks and conjurors had their public, whilst fortune tellers did a roaring trade, most of these being aged Lapp women. Thus did trade and swindling go on, eating and drinking everywhere, for the three days of the fair, and then the visitors returned to their homes for another year.

An Englishman named Hewitson visited the fair at Bjørn in 1833. There was life and gaiety around the booths, most of the dealers being respectable people. They had hung out the most startling display of clothes, towels and ribbons to tempt the female sex. Hewitson regretted that he could not talk of the *fair* sex, as that term would have been applicable to only one in every hundred. A quack offered them wonder cures, but the Englishmen preferred to drink coffee and punsch with the apothecary. Their boat's crew drank themselves drunk at the fair, and so the party had to spend the night in the little valley behind the fair ground, whence they looked across the straits at the beautiful mountain-range of 'The Seven Sisters.'

These fairs were a prominent feature in the lives of the people of Nordland, but modern means of communication rendered them superfluous and they gradually died out, Bjørn's fading away in 1882.

NOTES ON LOCAL HISTORY

The Province of Nordland embraces more than 250 miles of the coastline of North Norway and for convenience may be divided into four main districts, viz: Helgeland, Salten, Lofoten with Ofoten, and Vesteraalen.

Helgeland

This is the southernmost district in North Norway, which is entered when crossing the 65th parallel of latitude and stretches to the 67th, i.e. between Bindalsfjord and the promontory of Kunna. This latter formed the boundary between Helgeland and Salten, and its circumnavigation frequently held up north and south-bound traffic for long periods at a time in bad weather.

The ownership of much of the soil of Helgeland during the nineteenth century was vested in the 'Thomas Angell Stiftelse' —a wealthy Trondheim charity endowed under the will of an eighteenth-century member of the famous Angell family. Lorentz Mortensen Angell became the owner of Irgens Helgeland properties in 1678. He had migrated from Flensborg to Trondheim in about 1650 with his brother Morten, and had a daughter Rebecca who married Anders Dass, the son of the poet Petter. Lorentz Angell died in 1697 and his four sons agreed to the division of

136

10. Harbour at Bjørn on Dønna Island during a fair

11. Sawmills at Mosjøen c. 1875, with barques loading timber for Britain

his estate in 1703. Two of them, Lorentz and Peter, got the southern part of the property around Torget, Sømnes, Terraak, Rørøy and Hegge, whilst Hans' share passed to Anders Dass.

The eldest of the brothers—Albert—married Sarah, daughter of Thomas Hammond an immigrant Englishman. Albert had two sons Thomas and Lorentz who were both born in 1692. They were educated together at Copenhagen University, and lived for several years in Germany, Holland, England and Ireland. The father died when they were young, and when their mother died in 1717 they came home to Norway and launched big commercial ventures. Their firm became the largest in Trondheim, owning sawmills and timber yards, importing corn and groceries, and carrying on banking activities. They inherited many of the Angell properties in Helgeland, and shared their domestic life even after Lorentz married. The latter died in 1751, leaving an only daughter Karen, who married the famous Danish historian Suhm. He and uncle Thomas Angell could not get on together, so Thomas, who never married, bequeathed his fortune to charity in his will dated 1762. With this was founded that great and wealthy 'foundation' which is still called 'Thomas Angell's Stiftelse.' He died in 1767.

In 1802 the Foundation exchanged certain properties with the beneficiaries of Suhm's will, and thereafter held Vefsn, Alstahaug, Herøy and Brønnøy. But the most valuable part of the Foundation's property in the North was the royal tithes of Lofoten, Vesteraalen and Andenes. Owing to clauses in the will the estates were not broken up until 1890, when pressure of public opinion influenced their sale to the tenants in occupation. The rental from the Helgeland properties was not large and constituted only a small proportion of the income of the Foundation.

Terraak

This is the southernmost estate on the mainland, and became somewhat of a traffic centre when the North Norway Post was first sent by the overland route to Terraak in the early 1800's, the sea being used for further destinations.

Two Norwegians had promoted a timber company under the title of 'La Compania de Maderas' which exported timber to several Spanish cities, but was administered from Norway. In 1875 they acquired most of the forests round Bindal and Tosen fjords, but after ten years of felling these were exhausted and the company wound up. One of its principals—Frithjof Plahte—bought up the whole property, he being at the same time controller of many undertakings in the east of Norway and one of its principal industrialists. The forests were left untouched for several years, even prior to the export prohibition of 1892, and it was not until 1928 that their exploitation recommenced.

Tjøtta

This island home which had been of such importance in saga-times had a higher reputation for lavish hospitality than any other Nordland settlement during the nineteenth century, when the family of Brodtkorb were the owners.

The Spanish geologist, Vargas Bedemar, wrote in admiration of the manor-house at Tjøtta, which he considered the finest in all Nordland, and a German ornithologist F. Boie stated in 1817 that its doors were left open all night and guest rooms prepared for possible travellers. Nobody enquired as to the bona fides of visitors, and on one occasion Mr. Brodtkorb being anxious that a party should not leave before *he* wished them to, unshipped the boat's rudder and hid it.

An English tourist, Robert Chambers, arrived by the new steamer *Prinds Gustav* in 1840, together with the eldest son of the owner of Tjøtta. The old father, who looked like a 'Scottish Laird,' had studied at Edinburgh University. Chambers concludes: 'I left the shores of Tjøtta very sad at the thought that I should never see these dear people again.'

The great manorial estate was gradually broken up, and the last of the Brodtkorb's sold what remained to the State in 1929. Tjøtta began as the seat of a mighty plutocrat, then became Church property and later Crown lands. It passed through a long period of private ownership and has now reverted to the Crown.

Alstahaug and Belsvaag

Tradition lives on in these small twin settlements and they are cherished by every 'nordlending,' for here is kept alive the memory of Petter Dass and of his successor a century later—-Bishop Mathias Bonsach Krogh. Alstahaug was the least thinly populated district in all Helgeland until, in the 1850's, Sandnessjøen became the centre of communications for the Rana and Vefsn fjords and the outlying islands. A portion of Petter Dass's parsonage and his ancient church, as also the 'Bishop's Palace' at Belsvaag, still stand to whisper echoes of the words and works of the two men who were perhaps the greatest 'nordlendinger' that ever lived. The church and Dass monument are objects of reverence to coastal travellers as 'hurtigruten' sails past.

Vefsn and Mosjøen

The history of the forests of Vefsn through the last three hundred to four hundred years is the tale of how a vast area of virgin country has been brought under cultivation. The strenuous efforts of the early pioneers to procure a livelihood from the forests is an epic in itself. Then came transition from the patriarchal ownership of Anders Dass and his immediate successors, to be followed by a relentless capitalistic exploitation of the natural glories of the three Vefsn valleys.

It was in 1864 that two Englishmen carefully examined the forests of Vefsn and farther up Hattfjelldalen. The owner of these forests had endeavoured to persuade the Norwegian Government to acquire his holdings, but their fate was sealed when five British capitalists formed the 'North of Europe Land Co.' and purchased the whole of Hattfjelldalen, Susendalen, Fiplingdalen and part of Svenningdalen, for the insignificant sum of £22,050.

They erected a large sawmill on Halsøya off Mosjøen, and then the fjord and valleys bustled with activity. At Mosjøen, where the river runs into the fjord, there had been a little trading and a few craftsmen, but now in the harbour there were at all times a number of large ships that sailed mainly for Edinburgh, Aberdeen and Hull. Farmers left their holdings and went on forestry work, and a 'short view' was acted upon by everyone concerned. This was a most unfortunate undertaking, since no regard for forest preservation was exercised and slaughter of trees became indiscriminate. The peak of production was in 1883, but then work died away owing to lack of suitable timber.

The British Company handed over its interests to a new English Company in 1888 whose main purpose was to dispose of the assets. And in 1900 the State acquired all the Hattfjelldal lands and parcelled them out into one hundred and twenty-four farms.

Mo i Rana

It was not until the late 1700's that any settlement worthy of the name was established at Mo, which is a town that owes its development to one family, that of Meyer, who acquired the place in 1860, and founded a line of 'nessekonger' that controlled it till the 1920's. The first Meyer made Mo the economic centre for Rana Inland, bought from the peasants and Swedes everything they had to offer, and kept well-filled warehouses of all commodities required from the outer world. He found a market for no less than a thousand boats annually that had been built on the fjord, and initiated export of game (ptarmigan, etc.) to England and Germany. The town of Mo is the child of the Meyers who will never be forgotten there if and when it becomes the 'Sheffield of Norway' as the politicians plan that it shall.

The Dunderland Mine

At the turn of this century the numerous rich deposits of iron ore in North Norway were attracting great attention. Foremost among these were the extensive ore veins in Dunderlandsdal behind Mo, where Consul Persson (of Sulitjelma fame) and that great 'nordlending' Ole Tobias Olsen competed for the mining rights. Persson won, and sold Dunderland to the British 'Dunderland Iron Ore Co. Ltd.' who in the succeeding years built the railway to Storfoshei and erected the extensive plant there.

Nearly all the North Norway iron ore mines, which had been begun with such great hopes, suffered a more or less tragic fate. There was, however, still life in the Dunderland mine at the outbreak of war in 1914, and between the wars there were periods when it was operated. The State has now acquired the British rights and other assets.

Dønnes

There were few properties in North Norway that merited being graded as manorial estates, but among these that of Dønnes, on the north part of the island of Dønna, was pre-eminent. After playing a considerable role in mediaeval times, it was sold by Preben von Ahnen in 1675 to a member of the family of Tønder which had its origin in the town of that name in South Jutland. Dønnes was inherited by a girl of twenty in 1751, who that year married a young Trondheim military officer named Coldevin. In that name it descended until its sale in 1916 away from the family that had laboured, loved and laughed there for two hundred and forty years. And so was sundered a social and cultural tradition that had prevailed uninterruptedly since saga-times, and was unique in its survival into the twentieth century.

The ancient central section of the ancestral home was destroyed by fire in 1892. Its church, which was probably built by Paal Vaageskalm in the early part of the thirteenth century, is still standing, though heavily restored in 1866.

Lurøy

Lurøy, an island lying just south of the Arctic Circle, is of especial interest to Scots as being the home of a Norwegian branch of the family of Dundas. Anders Dass, son of the poet, had inherited the place through his wife Rebecca Angell, but the first Dass to live on Lurøy had also acquired it by marriage, and was himself the grandson of the brother of poet Petter. It was in the 1830's that this Lurøy branch reassumed the name of Dundas which the poet's father had brought over from Scotland in about 1630. Lurøy passed out of the family in 1922, but the youngest daughter of the last Lurøy Dundas bought it back again in 1943.

An apple orchard was planted here at the turn of this century, and the fruit ripened through a series of years—surely unique on the fringe of the Arctic Circle?

Meløy

Up till 1650 this was the centre of what was perhaps the largest group of estates in North Norway, having come into the hands of a Benkestok after the Reformation. The first of that name moved up here from West Norway, and founded a race of Nordland aristocrats that set the fashion and controlled much of its economy for centuries. Indeed there was Benkestok blood in nearly all the 'nessekonger' families of yesteryear, although the male line died out in the seventeenth century.

SALTEN

The promontory of Kunna, a danger-point for old-time coastal traffic, forms the southern limit of the ancient bailiwick of Salten, and just north of it lie the twin settlements of Inndyr and Gildeskaal. Both of these have an interesting past, but they have played no major role in the life of Nordland for very many years.

Inndyr

Here dwelt the feudal lord of Haalogaland, in exceptionally beautiful and luxuriant scenery, at various periods during the seventeenth century. One of these Danish lords, Knud Stensen, had been so reckless as to father a child by a female person he had brought with him from Denmark, and the pastor of Bodin publicized the scandal by refusing to marry them and generally exposing their misdeed. But Knud had good friends at Court and continued to live in princely fashion at Inndyr. The estate was sold by the State in 1666, and was acquired in 1679 by Thomas Hammond (an Englishman who had settled in Trondheim), but he held it for only a short while. It then returned to the State again and became the residence of the Lord-Lieutenant of Nordland in 1723. The old mansion was burnt down in about 1750 and no trace remains.

Gildeskaal

Inndyr lay within the parish of Gildeskaal, where stands a stone church dating probably from the thirteenth century. A decorative 'Amtmand's Chair' from the 1720's is in the church, which was magnificently furnished by three generations of pastors named Bruun, who were rectors between 1688 and 1804.

At Gildeskaal was born the poet Elias Blix, who gave North Norway its beautiful 'national' anthem. He died in 1902.

Kjerringøy

At the southern entrance to the Vestfjord lie two trading-places that played a great role in coastal communications before the advent of steamers. The craft crept up the coast to Kjerringøy and Grøtøy before making a dash across the open sea of the Vestfjord to Lofoten. Consequently there were sometimes as many as a thousand sailors stormbound for long periods at either of these places. Nowadays steamers sail direct from Bodø to Lofoten, but Kjerringøy still possesses relics of its lively commercial activities in bygone days, and is the most attractive and extensive old-time trading-place still standing.

Grøtøy

This was the last sheltered harbour on the old route to Lofoten, and few places in these parts possess such traditions and history as Grøtøy. The main stem of the famous Nordland family of Schøning dwelt in their mansion here—almost without a break for two hundred and fifty years.

Grøtøy was devastated by fire in 1912, and when the firm of Schøning went bankrupt in 1923 it spelt the end of all trading at Grøtøy.

Steigen

The historical interest of this place is largely owing to its having been the official residence of the Judge (lagmann) of Haalogaland through six hundred years—from the time of King Sverre until the abolition of the post in 1787.

It—and Skaanland nearby—was also a seat for many years of a branch of the distinguished family of Schønnebøl. The first Schønnebøl came out of Denmark as a poor man but had the good fortune to marry a Benkestok girl in 1565. Their principal seat was at Bertnes, a few miles from Bodøgaard, but before 1600 a Peder Schønnebøl was living at the judge's residence on Engeløy by Steigen.

Steigen has an ancient stone church on Engeløy, which was struck by lightning in 1657 and rebuilt the following year.

Hammarøy

Here was born the world-famous twentieth-century novelist Knut Hamsun. He served his apprenticeship at Tranøy on the northern tip of the island.

THE TOWN OF BODØ

One of the last major internal problems that the Dano-Norwegian Government had settled prior to the separation of the two countries, was the removal of the stranglehold that Trondheim—and to an even greater extent Bergen—had exercised over Nordland. In the years immediately preceding the outbreak of war with England in 1807 the trade of Nordland

12. Kaafjord, with its English church and the first steamer to ply round the coast of Finnmark

13. Kjerringøy, a well planned trading centre in days of sail

had flourished, and this prosperity revived ancient proposals for the establishment of a transit town in Nordland.

The idea was to create an entrepot for the trade between the White Sea and Western Europe, as well as to provide a centre for the export of fish from Lofoten—which at that time played a far greater part in Norway's balance of foreign trade than it does today. During the years of war (1807–14) the problem had been to keep alive trade with the Russian Arctic ports, and the dictates of emergency had forced the Government to decree three new laws during 1813, which were calculated to lead Nordland trade into an entirely new field.

In January 1813 Nordland's indebtedness to Bergen was considerably reduced by depreciation of the currency. In May came the decree 'concerning the foundation of a town in Nordland,' to be followed in October by a law enabling Nordland no longer to have its entire economy tied to Trondheim and Bergen.

On May 20, 1816, the new town of Bodø received its charter. It was sited at the small trading-place of Hundholmen, almost at the extreme tip of Bodø peninsula. Here in 1803 some Trondheim merchants set up a 'Trade and Fishery Establishment' with ambitious plans for whaling, fishing, trade and direct export abroad. When war came in 1807 the Company's large warehouses were used to store Russian corn, the stocks of which became of such value that an earthwork was erected on Nyholmen, and twenty to thirty guns mounted, with a garrison of two hundred men.

But Bodø made a bad start owing to desperate currency difficulties, falling prices, a cessation of foreign trade, unrest in Spain and Italy which were its principal markets, and finally the fantastic 'smuggling' case which has been known to historians as *The Bodø Affair*.

The Bodø Affair

This is of interest to Englishmen the world over, since the hitherto accepted Norwegian statement of the case casts a slur on prominent characters in English history and the fair fame of British diplomacy. The amazing chain of events reads like a novel, in parts indeed like a 'crook' story. It is an historical romance, the background of which was a reality that strung all its points together in a dramatic sequence, and far better than any writer of fiction could possibly have arranged them.

A British firm—Everth & Son—served as a catspaw for a London Banking House, and one side of Everth's business developed into providing cover for extensive smuggling and frauds on the Norwegian revenue.

In 1818 the Norwegians believed they had discovered the real nature of Everth's business, and his goods were confiscated by the Bodø customs. He thereupon recovered his goods by an armed raid on the customs warehouse, and made his escape to England. There he succeeded in setting British diplomacy in motion with a view to compensation. The Norwegians considered that the Swedish diplomats who were at that time conducting all Norwegian external affairs, had no direct interest in the Norwegian case and yielded to British diplomatic pressure without submitting the facts to a judicial enquiry. In 1821 these claims, which were unjust in Norwegian eyes, were settled by payment to the English traders of compensation amounting to £18,000. Thus much for the Norwegian point of view in the Bodø affair.

Smuggling was rife all over North Norway at this period, and there was an element of it in the transactions of this particular trader, but in British eyes his substantial trade was entirely legitimate. Indeed, at this period imports from Britain to Bodø were in the neighbourhood of £26,000 per annum. This new British trade development was resented by the merchants of Bergen and Trondheim, who had for so long enjoyed a monopoly of Nordland trade, and everything points to the fact that they indulged in a vindictive conspiracy to oust rivals from their 'Tom Tiddler's ground.' Thus much for the British point of view.

Broadly speaking the issue between Britain and Norway was that the latter regarded the criminal acts of a private individual as a matter for domestic jurisdiction, whereas the English believed that the high-handed Norwegian action resulted from a deep-laid and powerful conspiracy against British trade, which called for diplomatic intervention.

Everth's agent in the newly founded town of Bodø was named Gerss, a native of Finland of Swedish parentage. His opponents were the 'Hundholmen Company,' a Trondheim undertaking though the trade was mainly in the hands of Bergen merchants. This firm had not been very successful since it started operations in 1803.

No sooner had Everth's firm reconstructed buildings on Nyholmen—where they had been directed by the Lord-Lieutenant—with materials brought out from England, than Gerss received notice to quit. In 1817 a new Customs Inspector had been appointed to Bodø, and he despatched (most significantly from Bergen) an application to occupy the Government buildings which Gerss had just reconditioned. Gerss then made an offer to build any essential premises for the Customs Inspector on the mainland where his work lay, but was unable to obtain the cancellation of his threatened eviction from Nyholmen. So Mr. Everth, junior, sailed for Bodø on June 10, 1818, to deal with the difficulties on the spot.

With Everth's arrival in Norway the most exciting act of the drama begins, there being two points at issue, viz. eviction from Nyholmen and charges of smuggling.

A Mr. Stead invested £14,000 in goods purchased in Antwerp and London, to be sold in Norway and reinvested in fish. Everth's were the agents but the goods belonged to Stead. Everth wrote to Gerss begging him to get the cargo from the ship *Commerce* discharged before the Customs officer paid a visit, so Gerss set to work on the arrival of the ship to make the assistant Customs officer drunk, and locked him in his cabin. Twenty-two casks of molasses and rum were landed from the *Commerce*, but a quantity of tobacco and rum were confiscated by the new Customs inspector.

Young Everth left England in his ship (the *St. Johan*), but was wrecked on Røst on June 28, 1818. From Røst—some fifty miles from Bodø—he wrote to Stead regretting that he could not communicate with Gerss for fear that the latter's imprudence might send the Customs officers over to Røst to compel him to pay duties, 'and entirely defeat my hopes of saving you harmless in this venture.' It is impossible to follow the fortunes of the *St. Johan's* cargo, but a certain amount of smuggling seems to have taken place. However, a representative of the Norwegian Customs did arrive at Røst, and a considerable deposit appears to have been paid against possible duties.

The third ship—*Forsøget*—arrived at Bodø on August 10th, and Everth diverted her immediately to discharge her cargo to a friendly 'innkeeper' named Lorck at Storvaagan in Lofoten. Thereafter she was to assist in salvaging the goods from the wrecked *St. Johan*. Three of *Forsøget's* crew, however, went ashore and laid an information. Everth acted promptly by putting them on board one of Gerss' ships named *Oscar* and telling the captain to clear for England without papers, with a story of having been driven off the coast of Norway in a gale. Unfortunately a gale actually arose which drove the *Oscar* back to the very spot where the Bodø Customs inspector happened to be, and she was at once seized.

On September 24, 1818, Everth was arrested for resisting eviction. The Copenhagen agent of the London banking firm which was at the back of the whole business, wrote in January 1819 to the British Minister in Stockholm reporting the unwarranted arrest of Everth and requesting an investigation, and this the Minister promptly asked for. Then the matter became more serious since Everth's aged father died and the remaining partner committed suicide. The affairs of the firm were in confusion and Everth's presence in England became a matter of urgency. Although the firm was solvent at that time, Everth went bankrupt a few years later, so there appears to have been every justification for the action of the King of Norway-Sweden in March 1819, in setting Everth free for three months to enable him to visit England, on depositing security as bail against his return. On April 29th, however, the British Minister in Stockholm wrote to Lord Castlereagh: 'the conduct of Mr. Everth appears to have been such that it would be difficult to justify any further interference on his behalf on the part of this mission.'

In fact Everth had meanwhile secured his own release and taken steps to get out of Norway by high-handed methods. He

148

attacked the Customs House at Bodø with two boatloads of men from his ship *Commerce*, recovered the sails and rudder of his arrested schooner *Forsøget* and a large part of the confiscated contraband. He then sailed both his ships for home, carrying off the guard the authorities had posted at the warehouse, whom he later released in an open boat to make the best way they could back to land. Everth's official story of his 'snatch and grab' raid is filled with touches of humour, he making out that he took no violent action but that everything he wanted 'fell as it were into his mouth.' His letter to Stead, however, gives an entirely different and obviously more correct account of what took place.

There can be no doubt that Everth considered himself justified in his highest-handed action against the Customs inspector whom he regarded as an unmitigated scoundrel and, probably correctly, as being in the pay of commercial rivals.

It is almost certain that the whole affair was due to the machinations of the Norwegian Fishery interests, and indeed in a petition on behalf of Stead it is boldly stated as an incontrovertible fact that: 'it is but as yesterday the Government determined on a regular levy of Customs duties in Nordland.' This view, with an astute slurring over of the smuggling charges (which after all had not been judicially proved), was the one put forward in the memorial which was addressed to Lord Castlereagh on June 1, 1819.

This document is exaggerated, florid and verbose, but it was the first connected statement of the alleged facts to reach the British Government. The impression it made on the Foreign Office was certainly not too favourable, since Castlereagh's first instructions to the British Minister in Stockholm were not by any means a wholehearted championship of the cause of the British merchants.

The agent in Copenhagen, named Denovan, who was undeniably the villain of the piece, bribed a clerk in the Norwegian Finance Department to get hold of the papers from the Norwegian side. In the light of what he found there he reconstructed the whole claim by transferring practically all its items from Everth to Stead, the latter having been regarded throughout the whole proceedings as a wholly innocent sufferer—a character he succeeded in maintaining to the last.

And so representations were made on Stead's behalf, with the result that on October 27, 1819, the King of Norway-Sweden issued orders for the return of Stead's property. No demand for compensation was put forward by the British at this stage and, had the Norwegians promptly obeyed the instructions to return the property, the question of compensation would no doubt have been left to the Norwegian courts. Norwegian resistance to the King's order was founded, not on the manipulation of ownership from Everth to Stead, but on more or less technical grounds, in that his overriding the jurisdiction of the Norwegian Courts was *ultra vires*. This infuriated the British Foreign Office, it being their view that the King had pledged himself. Also since the foreign relations of the twin-kingdoms were administered from Stockholm they could not concern themselves with protests from Norway.

There were two further effects of the Norwegian recalcitrancy:

(*a*) By challenging the legality of what had been arranged in Stockholm they threw both the King and the Swedish Foreign Minister into the camp of their opponents.

(*b*) They so alienated the British officials that it became possible to induce them to get the claims for compensation, in addition to the mere minor matter of restitution, pressed through diplomatic channels.

Castlereagh and his subordinates became so unfavourably impressed by the obstinacy of the Norwegians that they saw the whole story of Everth, as well as the less obviously disputable claims of Stead, in a more favourable light.

The Swedes on their part accepted the British view that the Bodø of those days was a lawless place where no justice could be expected through the ordinary channels, and suspicion of North Norwegian justice was therefore shared by both negotiating parties. The Swedish Foreign Minister even pleaded that it was difficult, owing to poor communications and the laxity of the law, to enforce any orders north of Christiania.

Great Britain had begun to hint at threats to deprive both Norway and Sweden of the benefits of her reduced timber duties then in contemplation, and the results of such a policy might have been more serious to both countries than the Bodø affair was worth. And so on June 22, 1821, a settlement was reached in Stockholm whereby the English merchants received compensation amounting to £18,000.

What were really the rights of this case? We may agree with the Norwegian verdict so far as to admit that neither Everth nor Stead deserved to have one penny, and of course the criminality of Denovan is beyond question. But the case presents so many different points of view, and for Everth some sympathy must be felt. If his conduct was lawless his treatment was severe, and his belief in the jealousy of trade rivals was no doubt justified.

The British diplomats come in for severe censure by Norwegian historians, but it must be remembered that they had not the correspondence of the 'villains in the piece' before them, as these only came to light later. They were led to believe that Norwegian justice could not be trusted, and felt that Everth and Stead were really the victims of a conspiracy directed against British trade, on which basis the case for diplomatic pressure becomes a strong one.

The Norwegian claim that the whole affair was a matter for their domestic jurisdiction was well founded but, instead of reiterating and emphasizing this point, they made the mistake of relying on mere obstructiveness and showed a lack of diplomatic finesse.

The Swedes evinced a tendency to sacrifice justice for diplomatic expediency, and the Norwegians were technically right in condemning the manner in which the officials of Sweden handled their case. In the long run, however, the Swedes acted in the best interests of both countries, though in doing so they showed themselves indifferent upholders of the national honour of Norway.

Out of this minor incident arose the bitterest feelings in Norway towards Britain, but even more against Sweden. The national Press complained that Norwegians, who had just regained their independence, were receiving worse treatment from a great Power than it meted out to the negroes of West Africa. The Bodø Affair was certainly the greatest diplomatic incident in North Norway during the whole of the nineteenth century, and as late as 1905 was freely advanced in arguments for the independence of Norway.

Bodøgaard

This ancient house had been the seat of the Lords-Lieutenant of Nordland since Preben von Ahnen had taken up residence there in about 1660. It lay close to the parsonage near the ancient church of Bodin, and there are many tales of disputes between priest and feudal lord as neighbours. It was bought by the Hundholmen 'Trade and Fishery Establishment' in 1811.

When Leopold von Buch came this way in 1807 he expressed his surprise at finding such cultured and enlightened people in a spot so cut-off from the world as Bodøgaard.

Bodø History

Ten years after its foundation Bodø had a population of only 253, and in 1835 the Lord-Lieutenant reported that: 'although it is favourably situated in the central district of the province and has a good harbour, it is not likely to prosper owing to lack of hinterland and the difficulties of connections abroad. There is no overseas trade and no call for such.' Actually in the early days of Bodø foreign ships sailed by to Tromsø where freedom from Customs duties in their Russian trade gave openings for disposal of cargoes to foreign skippers that were far wider than the limited area that the port of Bodø tried to serve.

It was not until the 1860's that 'the silver harvest of the sea' attained fantastic proportions, and a corresponding accession of wealth and prosperity to the inhabitants of Bodø. It did not become a town worthy of the name until 1867. During ten years (1864–74) shoals of herrings (storsild) visited the whole coast of Nordland in fantastic numbers. They arrived each year at exactly the same date, which in Vesteraalen was during October, in Salten November 29th, and South Helgeland during December. People came here from all parts of Norway, and there was bustle and activity as never before, whilst numerous fortunes were made especially during the record catch of 1871. It was an extraordinary period when many people took to the sea who had scarcely heard of fishing. Shop girls and farm hands put their savings into boats and fishery concerns, and many who had lived in poverty became prosperous overnight.

But the herrings (storsild) vanished as quickly and unexpectedly as they had come. They were replaced, however, by shoals of 'fat' herring (fetsild) and good fishing seasons persisted until the turn of the century.

Bodø became a transit port for herring fishermen and buyers from all parts of Norway. In 1855 it had housed but 228 souls— 4,300 in 1896.

On top of the favourable local conditions came the establishment of the great undertaking at Sulitjelma, and Bodø was frequented by Swedish and Norwegian workmen on their journeys to and from the copper mine. There was a veritable 'gold-diggers rush' here during the last thirty-five years of the nineteenth century.

Bodø has, however, failed to fulfil the great hopes that led to its foundation, viz. to become the leading import and export harbour for the whole province of Nordland.

Sulitjelma

One day in 1866 a forester showed the storekeeper at Venset some shining stones somewhat larger than peas. The shopkeeper made haste to visit the place of discovery and carried away specimens for assaying the copper content. The report was so satisfactory that shopkeeper Koch at once registered his rights of ownership over distant Sulitjelma. Ten years later he commenced systematic investigations, but the problem of transporting the ore to the coast was so great that it was not until 1886 he found anyone bold enough to take the development

153

risks—a Consul Persson from Hälsingborg. Koch, the pioneer, died at his home in Venset in 1920, aged eighty-nine.

Actual mining operations began in 1887 under the Swedish Sulitjelma Mining Co. At first the ore was transported to the lake at Sjønstaa on a road the company built, but two years later a narrow gauge mountain railway was constructed, and this rail was opened for general traffic in 1896.

Such an isolated spot as Sulitjelma had perforce to be self-contained when the mining population increased so rapidly, so its present hospital was built in 1894 and its church in 1899.

Rognan

This spot has been a boat-building centre from a remote past. The larger craft are built on Rognan's shore but smaller boats, up to 55 feet in length, are put together as far as eight miles up the valley and are then floated down to Rognan when the river is in spate in the spring. If the river was too low they used to be driven or dragged down on rollers, each operation taking as much as a week. Saltdal is now a district of boat-builders, foresters and farmers.

Skjerstad

A Swede who passed this way in 1816 has left a vivid description of a Sunday at Skjerstad. The church, painted red with a steeple, lay on a birch-clad hill surrounded by yellow cornfields and green meadows. 'It was Sunday, and a crowd of people arrived in large boats, some having as many as thirty on board. Boats were scurrying to the landing-place from every direction. The menfolk, who as a whole looked far more attractive than the women, were a splendid lot of fellows. Most of them wore the costume of the Nordland fishermen—tall polished hat, wide trousers, half-boots, multicoloured scarves, and dark-grey pullover with blue collar that clung gracefully to the body and reached down over the hips. . . . The church was filled with people strolling aimlessly about before the service began. There were cries of children, snoring and whispering, with none of the reverence that is to be expected at a church service. . . .'

When the service was over people streamed out of the church and hurried each to his boat, pushed off and rowed away. It was a remarkable sight to see fifty boats filled with people racing in all directions from one spot all over the surface of the fjord.

The inhabitants of Saltdal and Skjerstad fjord are known as 'Saltvaeringer' and have other characteristics than those of the coastal dwellers.

LOFOTEN WITH OFOTEN

Before Narvik and Ofoten became absorbed into mining activities and international transport the site of the town was occupied by a modest farm or two. In the remainder of Ofoten, as in all the neighbouring fjords, there was only a sparse population. The products of its soil and forests were entirely for home consumption, while fishing provided the wherewithal for purchase of the slender imports from other parts of the country.

It was the invention of the 'Thomas' method of refining iron ore in 1878 that made possible the exploitation of the enormous deposits in north Sweden, and in the 1880's a British company obtained a concession to develop these and also to construct and operate a railway therefrom—eastwards to Luleaa and westwards to Narvik. The first manager, William Spear, had worked in the English factory at Brettesnes in Lofoten, and the fine stone offices he built at Narvik were nicknamed 'Speargaarden.' He got the reputation of being arrogant towards his employees, and during 'the English time' a company of soldiers had to be sent up from Trondheim to restore order. His high-handed actions were credited with having caused many breaches of the peace.

After a few years this company had to be wound up, and the Norwegian Government then acquired its properties on their side of the frontier. All work ceased until 1898, when the Norwegian and Swedish Governments agreed that each should construct its own section of 'The Iron Ore Railway between Narvik and

155

Luleaa.' A Swedish company—Luossavaare-Kirunavaare A/B (L.K.A.B.)—acquired a concession to develop the mines and it still operates them.

For a few short years the harbour was known as 'Viktoriahavn,' having been so named by the British after their Queen. On their departure Narvik, the old name of the farm on the site, was adopted by the Storting.

In addition to its enormous transit traffic in ore westwards, there is a considerable throughput of *fresh* fish from Lofoten, using rapid transport via the Swedish railway network to the markets of Europe.

Skrova

This island juts out into the Vestfjord, and was the first objective that sailing craft made for after leaving Grøtøy for Lofoten. It was for many years perhaps the most frequented of all Lofoten fishing harbours, but has now faded into insignificance. Two of the ancient dwelling-houses, however, still stand as souvenirs of bygone prosperity, though its mediaeval church ceased to exist in about 1600.

Brettesnes

It lies on the island of Store Molla, and opposite to the little Kjefsøy where the 'ting' was held in saga-times. It was a considerable fishing village from which some eighty boats were operating in 1835.

In 1879 a British company, trading under the name of 'Jensen & Co.,' bought Brettesnes. They established a fish-treating factory and built houses for their workers that are standing today. Older residents in Svolvaer remember the excitement when news came that a British ship had entered Brettesnes. Their mothers rowed the short distance to buy household articles which were at that time unobtainable from suppliers up north—such as fine linen, chinese porcelain, etc. Many of these old-time purchases can still be seen in the homes of Svolvaer. In 1892 production ceased and the English personnel returned home, but work was resumed in 1902 by the English firm 'All Rich Guana Co.' That company ceased operations after twelve months, and Brettesnes passed under Norwegian ownership in 1912.

Svolvaer

This main cod fishing centre has a few traditions behind it. As late as 1760 it was Crown land, but at least two families of traders are known to have operated here in the early part of the seventeenth century. Its good harbour and central position in the Archipelago have made it the chief port in the Lofoten Islands.

It was in the 1890's that *Miss Caroline Harvey* of Tenby in Wales, first came to Svolvaer as a tourist. Her sympathy for the fishermen in their hard struggle with nature caused her to spend part of every summer there, and to devote considerable sums from her ample fortune upon schemes to make the lot of the fishermen more agreeable. When the Seamen's Mission Hotel was built at Svolvaer she was a generous contributor, and many an entertainment of a strictly temperance nature was arranged at her instance. In 1895 she presented a life-saving vessel named *Svolvaer* to the Royal Norwegian Lifeboat Society.

Caroline Harvey died in 1932 and, at the request of the Community of Svolvaer, the Norwegian Minister in London attended her funeral at the family chapel at Langley, Herts, to deposit wreaths from her numerous friends in the faraway Lofotens. Svolvaer has honoured her memory by naming the road round its outer harbour 'Caroline Harvey's vei,' whilst the small boat in which she rowed herself out to spend countless days amongst her beloved fisherfolk, is now housed in the Fram Museum at Oslo.

Kabelvaag

This was the centre of the Lofoten fisheries for 1,000 years or more. It embraces the ancient fishing centres of *Storvaagan* and *Finneset*, over whose roofs the modern statue of the twelfth-century King Øiestein now gazes down from his hilltop. The place teems with centuries of history, but neighbouring Svolvaer and Henningsvaer have stolen much of its material prosperity away.

Henningsvaer

This cluster of islets has attracted fishermen to its naked rocks and snug coves ever since the Reformation, and perhaps even earlier.

A firm of manufacturing chemists in London had for many years operated a cod-liver oil boiling plant here, their representative being an elderly Englishman named Hawes. Mr. Hawes was trapped in the Lofotens when the German occupation started, and spent a few months in Kabelvaag gaol as a prisoner of the Germans. When the cod-fishing season began in February 1941 he was released for the period of the fisheries to supervise his factory on German account. On that exciting morning of March 4th his boy ran into the house calling: 'There are English soldiers outside!' Mr. Hawes believed this to be some impish trick, but none the less rose and on looking out of the door was addressed in broad Yorkshire dialect by a helmeted soldier in British uniform. And thus was effected the 'Lofoten Raid' on Henningsvaer, simultaneously with those on Svolvaer, Stamsund and Brettesnes.

VESTERAALEN

Hadsel

This island was visited by numerous British sportsmen during the nineteenth century. The Rev. Frederick Metcalfe, who wrote *The Oxonian in Norway*, called the island 'Rypeø' (Ptarmigan island).

Hadsel Church near Stokmarknes has a long history.

Melbu

In Viking times there was a large estate here on the south side of the island of Hadsel. In 1830 a Coldevin from Dønnes bought the property and built a fine mansion—part of which still stands—

that was said to be the largest north of Trondheim. He astonished the neighbours by installing a water supply in the building, which at that time was unknown in any Nordland dwelling.

Metcalfe stayed here in 1855 when the widow Coldevin was châtelaine. He wrote: 'As usual an enormous number of strapping male and female domestics are to be found about the premises. To see them sit down to their meals, and the quantity of food they consume, is most astonishing.' He realized, however, that the widow, being both trader and farmer, required a very large staff.

Metcalfe was amazed at the culture in the house at Melbu, whose daughters could not only run the house but all play the piano and were expert dancers. Though there was a quiet purposeful air about them, their native gentleness and good humour always made them delightful companions.

Captain Molyneux of the British Navy shot here for many years, and painted the house he built in the 1890's a startling blue. It is still known locally as 'The Blue Castle.'

During the Second World War the collaboration of the 'nessekongen' with the Germans secured him privileges to erect the most modern fish-treating plant in the North. This is now operated by the State.

Sortland

This place supposedly lies in the heart of the ancient district of Aamd (Omd), the home of Karle and Gunnstein who made the 'Bjarmelandsferd' with Tore Hund in the eleventh century. It has been a centre of population for countless ages, since the ocean fishing banks lie close to the coast here and so it was but a short sail for the fishermen. Sortland also possesses fertile soil and a comparatively mild climate.

Andenes

Here on the northern tip of Andøya there has been a fishing centre since the Stone Age. It lies at the uttermost end of the modern Province of Nordland.

PART VIII

THE PROVINCES OF TROMS AND FINNMARK IN THE NINETEENTH CENTURY
1814–1905

THE PROVINCE OF TROMS

MALANGEN Fjord divides the bailiwick of Tromsø from that of Senja, and many authorities believe that the northern limit of Norwegian settlement was at Malangen in saga-times. In the history of Norwegian settlement the bailiwicks of Senja and Tromsø have ever been frontier lands. It is in these areas that Norwegians have at all times come into contact with people of other races—Lapps, Russians and Kvens. Waste spaces and the coast of the Arctic Ocean provided the venue for hunting and fishing, and the resultant trading yielded profits far in excess of what was customary farther south.

Up to the close of the seventeenth century the deep fjords in Troms were referred to as 'Lapp-fjords.' The Reformation and other factors, however, caused a loss of markets for fish, so the fishermen were compelled to migrate inland, to clear the forests and make the earth yield whatever the harsh Arctic climate would permit. Cultivation of the soil has taken a very secondary place to hunting and fishing in these parts, and hence their story through the ages is but the hundredfold repetition of the habits of fish, of those of the men who caught them, and of the buyers and their markets.

Bjarkøy

The ancient history of Bjarkøy and Trondenes has been told elsewhere in this volume. Bjarkøy was referred to in the sixteenth century as 'the Rosenkrantz property' since it had then belonged to Erik Rosenkrantz, the famous viceroy at Bergen. Later it was

14. A "Nordlandsjekt"

15. Skrova 'hall,' where trees grow despite Atlantic gales

16. Loppa, where Prince Alfred of England stayed in 1862

acquired by Preben von Ahnen, whose son Iver succeeded to it in 1675. His wife was Maria, sister to Lillienskiold the excellent Lord-Lieutenant of Finnmark who was author of *Spectrum Boreale*. Iver died in 1722 when it passed away from that family, and now no visible relics remain of its former glories.

Trondenes

Near to its mediaeval church lies the nineteenth-century town of Harstad, but on its seaward side stands the manor-house of Røkenes, whose history is documented since 1350, when Gunnar gave a portion of the estate to Trondenes for the good of his soul.

Ibbestad—Hamnvik

As recently as the 1880's the white walls of the old stone church of Ibbestad were still standing. But its landing-place lay too exposed to gales and so it faded out in favour of Hamnvik in about 1795. In that year Louis Philippe stayed a while in the trader's house which had then just been completed, and that still stands. He later presented a portrait which hangs here yet.

Few places in these parts have retained so much of their original character as has Hamnvik.

Kløven (Klauva)

Here in the south-east corner of Senja Island was the centre of trading and social life in Senja bailiwick during the nineteenth century. At its close the place faded out and has ceased even to exist, all its functions having passed over to Finnsnes on the opposite shore of the entrance to Gisundet. Finnsnes flourishes as the port of the Maalselv and Bardu valleys, and has good road connections with Troms inland.

Bentsjord

Long before the town of Tromsø on its island became a centre of traffic, the trading-place at Bentsjord on the east shore of

Rystraummen was a thriving settlement whose owner controlled the lives of the few residents in Malangen and Balsfjord, as well as on the islands to seaward.

First mentioned in 1567, Bentsjord is certainly even older, and it played the dominant part in the restricted economic life of southern Tromsø through more than three hundred years. But its trade was appropriated by Tromsø in the 1820's, and before the close of last century its considerable properties had been disposed of piecemeal. The ancient mansion-house, and the splendid main building of 1824, indicated the status of their owner as a landed proprietor, since the local trade could not have been sufficient to support a dwelling of such proportions.

The last farms were sold off in 1920, and the buildings at Bentsjord razed to the ground. Thus was destroyed a great tradition in a part of Norway where there is little tangible evidence of the culture of other days.

HISTORY OF TROMSØ

The quarter of a century that followed the Napoleonic Wars was a typical post-war period. Several of Norway's chief exports such as fish and timber had great difficulties to overcome, and exchange value of its currency fell desperately. This period was therefore marked by much unrest and stagnation and it was a long time before any marked improvement set in. Tromsø, however, in striking contrast to other Norwegian towns, experienced a remarkably rapid and healthy growth in the years following 1814. This was not solely due to the resumption of a brisk trade with the White Sea ports, but even more owing to its new connections with overseas markets.

In 1819 the first ship from London arrived at Tromsø. It was the barque *Elia*, which aroused great excitement since she was the largest vessel that had ever anchored in the harbour. After loading at Hammerfest she returned to Tromsø to load stokkfish, and carried her consignments to the Mediterranean. This initiated a new era in the history of the town since it reopened export to the Latin lands, and that trade continued to flourish bringing much prosperity to Tromsø.

The small Russian vessels came in large numbers, but export southwards henceforward far exceeded that to the east, and the disproportion continued to grow. The harbour in the 1820's was frequented by numbers of vessels from England and France, the former country gladdening the hearts of the Norwegians by sending quantities of 'porter,' whilst France sent claret and brandy.

A new line of activities was started in 1821 through hunting and fishing in the Arctic Ocean. The first area to be covered was Bear Island, where good hauls of walrus were made. In 1826 Spitsbergen began to be visited, and Arctic Ocean activities have continued ever since those early days as a regular branch of Tromsø's commercial life.

Imports from England included salt, manufactures, groceries, etc., the exports being dried fish and cod-liver oil. Bodø exported almost as much fish as Tromsø whilst Hammerfest sent out six times as much. The reason for Tromsø's poor showing was that Senja and Tromsø bailiwicks had not been granted the privilege of free trade in Russian imports.

Finnmark's Lord-Lieutenant reported in 1827 that Tromsø, despite the difficult times, had successfully competed with Bodø and Hammerfest, although those two ports profited by exemption from taxation and a low scale of customs duties, whereas Tromsø paid full duties. He considered that the reasons for Tromsø's progress were plain. In the first place, unlike Bodø, it was not situated in the middle of Bergen's trading area, and, secondly, it carried on trade with Russia, with which country Bergen had no concern. It was more advantageous for producers in the surrounding districts to send goods to Tromsø than through middlemen to Bergen. Tromsø was also far more independent of Bergen than was Nordland proper, since it procured most of its necessities from Russia.

Summer fishing in Finnmark brought life and trade to Tromsø, whilst foreign shipping elected to sail past Bodø and call at Tromsø, where their skippers could be certain of doing business not merely for local consumption but also for the barter trade with Russians. He also mentions Tromsø as a centre for the fur trade with Russia, not merely for furs obtained locally but many, especially red fox, were sent from Germany via Bergen to be sold to Russians at Tromsø.

A decisive change in trade with Russia took place in 1828, since for the ensuing eleven years Tromsø was on an equal footing with the two Finnmark towns—Vardø and Hammerfest. As late as 1815 articles of food value from Russia had been landed free of duty at Tromsø, but in 1816 duties were again levied on imported Russian flour. These duties were a burden on a young town, and so its merchants petitioned for reduction of duties on flour and corn—but without result. A Commission was, however, appointed, which reported complaints that Norwegian shipping had to pay duties in Russian ports that far exceeded those levied on Russians in Norway, and that the export of corn was permitted only to a limited extent and for short periods at a time. The recommendations of this Commission were embodied in the Commercial Treaty signed at St. Petersburg in February 1828. By it the Norwegian Government agreed to exempt from customs duties flour, corn, hemp, rope work, tar and building materials that had been imported from harbours in the White Sea to 'Finmarken.' By this word the Norwegians had intended Finnmark proper, whilst the Russian Government maintained the provisions of the Treaty covered the whole Province of Finnmark, and therefore included the bailiwicks of Senja and Tromsø. Out of concern for good neighbourly relations the Norwegian Government agreed to the Russian interpretation. The Treaty was to run for six years and so a new treaty was concluded in 1834, whereby exemption from customs duties was continued for the whole province till 1839. After that the Norwegian Government would no longer permit free trade from Senja and Tromsø, and in the Commercial Treaty of April 1838 between Norway-Sweden and Russia, only Finnmark proper was exempt from duties on Russian products.

Those years of free Russian trade (1828–39) gave a considerable stimulus to Tromsø and made a great contribution to the growth and prosperity of the town, its population increasing ten-fold between 1807 and 1835. Stabilization of currency also was of vital importance to its progress.

It was a great loss to Tromsø when the business of handling Lofoten fish was transferred to more southerly towns. Bodø had been moribund until the 1860's when it began to flourish, largely at the expense of Tromsø. Harstad also lay in a district which had for long traded with Tromsø, but in 1861 the former town took its local trade away.

And so it was that the Finnmark fisheries came to be the main source of Tromsø's prosperity, and its inhabitants fished and traded there year after year in ever-increasing numbers—especially in East Finnmark. Indeed, on a single day in 1864 no less than 300 boats sailed through Tromsøysund on their way to the Finnmark fisheries.

Emigration began on a large scale in the 1860's. The heaviest year was 1864 when between 500 and 600 'nordlendinger' took ship at Tromsø direct to Quebec. In 1873 numbers went to Queensland from Tromsø, and in the following year to New Zealand and Australia.

It was in the autumn of 1868 that the celebrated 'storsildfisket' (full-grown herring fishery) began, which was soon to awake all of ancient Haalogaland into feverish activity. Then came the Franco-Prussian War to maintain the wave of speculation and splendid conditions for export. But reaction came in 1874 when bankruptcies were numerous.

The rich shoals of herrings that appeared off the Baahuslen coast of Sweden in 1877 resulted in a catastrophe for Tromsø. A spate of bankruptcies occurred there which led to an acute crisis. The following year saw a number of forced auctions, and distress spread far and wide. That depression lasted more than two years, during which the 'American Fever' raged once again, with emigration at distressingly high figures.

The tide turned again in 1884, and although Tromsø had by then lost its active trade and its own shipping, it still retained its status as an export town. In one particular sphere—Arctic hunting—Tromsø registered steady progress.

It was in 1884 that the first large English tourist ship—the *Ceylon* of 2,300 tons—came to the North Cape, to be followed next year by the Wilson liner *Domino*. These were the earliest special cruises from Britain, they initiating a tourist traffic that has since brought considerable wealth to North Norway.

In a story of Tromsø some reference is necessary to certain of the Arctic discoveries made by hunters sailing from that town. They began to be made about 1850 when seal-hunting in these areas started in earnest. Important details concerning the eastern parts of the Spitsbergen Archipelago were reported, and Frantz Joseph Land discovered. They explored the Kara Sea, the West Siberian Sea, and the waters off Greenland's east coast. From this immense area of ocean—from Taimyr Land in 94° East (close to Asia's north point at Cape Tsjeltuskini) to East Greenland in 25° West—they procured a mass of data concerning the geography and climate of the Arctic lands and seas, depths, oceanography and ice conditions.

Karnes

Tromsø Bailiwick was part of the Crown lands that Irgens bought from the King in 1666. It passed as a whole to the Dutch Baron de Petersen in 1683: i.e. virtually everything between Malangen Fjord and the boundary of Finnmark.

A Michael Hvid was appointed manager of this Tromsø property in 1716, and continued to act as agent to his own son Johan, who bought the Baron's property from his grandchild in 1751. Michael Hvid lived at Karnes in Lyngen from about 1730 until his death in 1757, and managed the considerable estate from that remote spot, which lies about a mile south of Lyngseidet. That narrow isthmus between Ullsfjord and Lyngenfjord has ever been traversed by a track that continues south along the shore of Lyngenfjord, up to the market-place of Skibotn and so over the mountains to Swedish Lappmark. The postal service had used that route from the 1690's.

Finds from the Stone Age have been made at Karnes, which without doubt was a place of sacrifice in heathen times. As a result of Thomas von Westen's labours a church was built there in 1731. Many legends survive of extraordinary people and happenings in the old house of Karnes during the eighteenth century.

Lyngseidet has now become the centre for the surrounding district, and the Karnes of bygone plutocrats now sleeps peacefully in its exceptionally beautiful natural surroundings.

Lyngen

Time and again numbers of Kvens have left their Finland to settle down in Finnmark and Troms. The route of entry into Troms was usually Skibotn, since the market-road there had been traversed from time immemorial. The Kvens came in waves during wars, or years of crop failures in their homeland. On occasions the magnet was a season of good fishing on the Norwegian coast. The Great Northern and Napoleonic Wars caused considerable migration, whilst a new stream arrived in 1832–33. But never did so many enter Norway as between 1865 and 1868. On that occasion they were destitute refugees from North Finland who could no longer scratch a bare living there and were obviously in extreme poverty. They crossed the frontier to avoid death by starvation.

Many settled down at Lyngen, and they were in such numbers that even the Norwegian language began to disappear. This created many problems in administrative, judicial and ecclesiastical affairs. But the immigrants proved to be remarkably virile and capable, pioneering on a grand scale in the northern parts of Troms inland.

Hamnes

There lived here in the early eighteenth century a remarkable man, Holger Danifer, whose father's life-story links Hamnes with the Dano-Swedish war of 1658. When Danifer, the loyal Dane, was (strange as it may seem) acting as guard on board a Swedish vessel laden with foodstuffs and a number of Danish prisoners of war, he overpowered the Swedish officers and crew and sailed into the closely invested city of Copenhagen, where his exploit fired the morale of the besieged—the more so since he brought news of the approach of a Dutch fleet whose purpose was to free Denmark. The old man gained high honours but little wealth, and this latter perhaps explains why one of his sons settled in remote Hamnes.

A remarkable lady named Ovidia Lyng (always referred to as 'Mother Lyng') took over Hamnes on the death of her second husband just after 1815, and ruled here like a queen till she died in 1848, aged eighty-two. Ovidia had twelve children of her own but nevertheless adopted thirty-two besides, and each of her family of forty-four was given a good start in life. The wheel-chair she used in her last days is still preserved here.

THE PROVINCE OF FINNMARK

The Crimean War broke out in 1854, and Britain and France blockaded the White Sea throughout that summer. They, how-ever, magnanimously permitted a barter trade between the inhabitants of Finnmark and White Sea Russians, whilst the Czar for his part agreed to a sufficient export to provision the fishing villages of Norwegian Finnmark. In August the Com-manding Officer of the patrolling Norwegian squadron was informed that the blockading force would allow small Norwegian vessels to sail to and from the White Sea if they were provided with papers signed by captains of Norwegian men-of-war declaring that their purpose was to provision Finnmark.

The blockade was called off in the autumn, but the English Commanding Officer was censured for leaving his station so early in the winter. In the following year—1855—a blockade was again established, and was not lifted till mid-October.

WEST FINNMARK

Loppa

When the coastal steamer sails round the promontory of Brynilen it enters the Province of Finnmark, and to seaward lies the small island of Loppa—the Mecca of several British sportsmen in the latter half of the nineteenth century.

In 1847 a much-travelled Norwegian inherited Loppa, and ruined himself by building a luxurious dwelling-house there. It

168

was then purchased by a Tromsø merchant who put in as manager G. P. Ulich, whose mother Margaret had come from Scotland in 1820. The owner advertised shooting rights on Loppa in the British Press, and the first English tenant was named White. He was so satisfied with the sport (ptarmigan, etc.) that, when passing through Tromsø on his way home, he gave authority to a lawyer there to arrange a long lease. The lawyer's knowledge of English was limited, so Mr. White returned next year to discover that he had purchased the *freehold* of Loppa island.

Margaret Ulich lived with her son, and had no difficulty in persuading the various English owners to lease the island, except shooting rights, to him. There were often parties of as many as seven Englishmen throughout the summer, Queen Victoria's second son, Prince Alfred, being a guest in 1862. The last of these visits was made by the famous African explorer Frank Linsly James in his yacht *Lancashire Witch* in 1887, when Loppa belonged to a Captain Ames of the Life Guards, who for many years had the distinction of being the tallest officer in the British Army. He sold the island to Ulich in 1890.

Øksfjord and Philippa Temple

Just round the next cape from Loppa island lies the 'fiskevaer' Øksfjord, where Marcus Buck was 'nessekongen' in the 1870's. He had a grand-daughter named Philippa, whose father Philip Harbroe Schwensen was a member of the Talvik family of that name. Philip H. Schwensen moved to Sørøya in 1843, was made sheriff there in 1859, and it was at Hasvik on Sørøya that Philippa Schwensen was born. Her mother died when she was a child and so she spent most of her girlhood with her grandfather at Øksfjord.

When Philippa—whose pet-name was Philene—was about seventeen she was staying with an uncle at Elvenes when a small English yacht named *Annie* arrived. On board were two brothers named Temple—of a Worcestershire county family—one of whom, George Theodore, was a lieutenant in the British Navy. It was a case of love at first sight, and their engagement was solemnized before the yacht left.

169

Lieutenant Temple was then sent on foreign service for five long years, and during all that time the two lovers wrote each other every week. So Temple's parents, who moved in the highest circles in London, seeing that it was a serious matter and fearing that their precious son was about to make a *mésalliance* with some fisher girl of no education, sent out the old family lawyer to report upon Philene. He found that she was not merely a captivating blonde but, having been educated in Trondheim, could hold her own in any society in the world.

So Philene lived on with her grandfather at Øksfjord until Lieutenant Temple came to claim her after their five long years of waiting. They were married. Temple resigned his commission to take up a business career in order to provide for them, and they brought up a large family in England. In Norway there is a tradition that she acted for her brother-in-law as Vicereine in Calcutta when he was acting-Viceroy, but that story cannot be substantiated, alas!

In all her London society life Philene never forgot Øksfjord, and when she was describing banquets and luxuries to her Finnmark relatives she used to say: 'They are nothing to me compared with eating sour milk in Vassdalen' (the name of the seter-hut of Øksfjord).

Philene died in 1924, and her husband Lieutenant-Commander Temple, R.N., a Commander of the Order of St. Olav, in 1935 at the age of eighty-eight.

The novelist Marie Corelli heard this story when on a tourist trip to the North Cape, and upon it based her best-of-all-sellers *Thelma*, or *The Norwegian Princess*—which was reprinted in 1936 in its sixtieth edition. Marie Corelli obviously traversed the ground that Philene trod when a girl, since she sets her scenes in such places as Alta, Talvik, etc.

Talvik

In the days of the 'octroi' Talvik was the centre for the so-called Alten trade, the place where Alta river salmon was shipped and trade with the Lapps carried on. It has been praised by many travellers for its charming situation and excellent harbour.

It was here that Marie Elizabeth Noodt lived in 1821, of whom Capell Brooke wrote that she was created 'to adorn a Court.'

Kaafjord

The outstanding feature at Kaafjord today is its church, which was erected by the British Mining Company there more than one hundred years ago to serve the needs of its employees. The church has many distinctive English features and, although a timber building, bears no relation architecturally to any other church in Norway. It is still standing, having miraculously escaped destruction when the Germans were devastating everything around.

Two Englishmen—John Rice Crowe and H. D. Woodfall—were the founders of Kaafjord's copper mine, which began production in 1826. Crowe had come to Norway after Waterloo, and first settled at Hammerfest, where he owned warehouses and traded at Fuglenes across the bay from that town. Woodfall of Kaafjord was a foundation member of the 'Tromsø Citizens Club' in 1821, and also a guarantor in 1836 of the 'Tromsø Savings Bank'—founded that year as the first bank in North Norway. Another British subject in Kaafjord when, or soon after, it began production was a Glaswegian, Charles Robertson, who became the progenitor of the Finnmark family of that name which is held in such honour there today.

The copper ore was exported direct to England, the skilled workmen being mostly Norwegians brought up from Røros and Folddalen. There were also some British apprentices. In 1829 there was already a population of 251, and forty houses had been erected. The mine, even in its earliest days, proved a blessing to the surrounding district. It became one of Norway's most important mines and the English company, which was floated in 1833 as Altens Kobbervaerk, earned handsome profits for a number of years.

In a letter Crowe wrote in 1843 he says that before Kaafjord mines were opened the north part of Finland and the Torneaa district had experienced a series of crop failures, which caused the inhabitants to resort to bark bread. Therefore they welcomed

171

the chance of work that the opening of the mines offered. For a long time he had employed as many as five hundred Kvens.

Crowe also stated that before the Kvens came, and when wages were almost twice as high as those of later times, no more than five local inhabitants could be persuaded to sign on at the mines, although they frequently went short of food and the work was of such a nature as to later be carried out by Kven women and children. He praised the Kvens as being alert, industrious and thrifty people.

The Lord-Lieutenant reported in 1860 that: 'Kaafjords or Altens, and Kvaenangens Copper Mines are still producing, but no fresh workings are being opened up. Since 1857 the two mines have belonged to the same company under the name of Altens and Kvaenangens Mine.' He also stated that Kvaenangen was paying its way, but Altens production was falling off; 291 workers were employed in 1860, and 1,098 people in the district were obtaining their livelihood from the mines—of whom 17 were British subjects.

In 1873 there was but one mine working in all Finnmark, namely that at Kaafjord. All activities there ceased long ago.

Kaafjord is a sacred place to all the Western world, for it was here that the German battleship *Tirpitz* was lying when British midget submarines crept through the nets and damaged her, almost irretrievably, at a critical phase of the war.

Bossekop

Long before the official market was moved from Elvebakken to Bossekop in 1844 the latter place had been an assembly-place. Schnitler wrote in 1744: 'Norwegians, Kvens and Lapps, who live in forests and among mountains, have their fish sheds and booths there.' It has been for many years the principal Lapp market in all Finnmark.

Elvebakken

Here at the old building of Altengaard, lying at the mouth of the Alta River, lived the King's Lieutenant for Finnmark from about 1740 until his headquarters were moved to Tromsø in 1814. Altengaard was burnt to the ground by the Germans in 1944, as also was the house of Jøraholmen, in which three generations of Dukes of Roxburgh had spent their summers fishing in the Alta.

Generations of British anglers have fished in the Alta River, the most notable in recent years being the Duke of Westminster, who pays a substantial sum yearly for the rights after Midsummer's Eve. The revenue accruing from this source to public funds has been of considerable benefit to the Alta community.

Hammerfest

There has been a trading centre here for centuries. A sketch by Lilienskiold at the close of the 1600's shows trees on the hillside opposite the church, but no timber now grows in the vicinity. Hammerfest has the distinction of being the most northerly town in the world, and possesses the largest and safest harbour in all West Finnmark. It was used, especially during the 'octroi' period, by vessels wintering up north. It was in 1787 that Hammerfest was granted its Royal Charter, and became recognized as a 'town,' though it remained such only in name for a number of years. It is now the 'capital' of West Finnmark.

An Englishman, John Rice Crowe, settled down in little war-battered Hammerfest in 1820, and bought the business premises at Fuglenes across the harbour from the town. Six years later he and Woodfall opened up the copper mine at Kaafjord, and floated a British company to take it (as also his Fuglenes business) over in 1833.

One of Crowe's British assistants at Kaafjord, Charles Robertson, bought the Fuglenes part of the concern from the new company in 1835, and in a couple of generations they had made it the most prosperous firm in Hammerfest, with branches all over Finnmark. Charles Robertson married a girl from Kristiansund, and his essentially British surname is now spread far and wide in Norway.

Details of life in Hammerfest in the 1820's can be read in

Capell Brooke's writings, he having much to say about his fellow-Englishman Crowe. The latter later married a girl from Djupvik in Altafjord, which caused her Norwegian adorer to emigrate in melancholy. Crowe was later appointed Vice-Consul at Hammerfest and kept a watchful eye on Russian aggressive intentions regarding Finnmark in mid-nineteenth century. He later became Consul-General in Kristiania, where he died in 1875 having played a unique and praiseworthy role in Anglo-Norwegian relations through fifty years.

The destruction of Hammerfest by the Germans at the close of the Second World War was one of their most thorough devastations. All that remained standing in the town were the walls of its mortuary chapel.

Maasøy

History has little to tell in this small fishing village, but Lilienskiold gave us a sketch of it just prior to 1700. The pastor of the parish was moved here from Ingøy in 1746, and the church followed him the year after. They made a habit of transporting churches in early days, for the same church was carried off to Havøysund in 1832 and returned to Maasøy in 1865!

But Maasøy's only claim to fame is that it housed Louis Philippe in the home of the trader there in 1795.

Scurvy was the curse of these lonely places where no vegetables could be produced. There are many references to its frequency on Maasøy.

Honningsvaag

This place is now the traffic centre for the North Cape area and Porsangerfjord, having supplanted nearby Kjelvik in about 1870. Kjelvik had a considerable Russian trade and it was evacuated for a while during the British blockade of 1809. It was at Kjelvik that the mother church for the fishing stations on the Arctic Ocean stood—the last of these churches here having been blown away by a tornado in 1882.

Store and Lille Tamsøy are celebrated as being the richest seabird egg and eiderdown islands in all Norway, whilst their swampy soil teems with cloudberries (moltebaer). King Christian IV on his voyage in 1599 was so impressed that he ordered close seasons to be observed there—a decree which has been faithfully observed ever since. Lilienskiold was enthusiastic about the natural wealth of Tamsøy, and in 1744 Schnitler names countless varieties of sea birds that frequented the place.

Numbers of boys and girls visit Tamsøy in the autumn to pick cloudberries on its spacious 'vidda.' They are sold fresh under the registered mark 'Tamsøymulter.'

Banak, at the head of Porsangerfjord, lies at the road junction for Karasjok, and has become an important traffic centre.

Svaerholt possesses the most frequented bird-mountain in all Finnmark, where as many as 10,000 eggs for preserving were collected annually in days long gone by. In about 1800 Amtmann Sommerfeldt refers to Svaerholtklubben as 'such a remarkable sight that in my opinion its praises should be sung by our finest poets.' Klubben is on the boundary of the two administrative areas of West and East Finnmark.

EAST FINNMARK

Laksefjord

On its eastern shore lies Lebesby with its church. It is a nineteenth-century settlement and has no history, except that it gave birth to a remarkable soothsayer whose forecasts are recited over all Finnmark as 'the prophecies of the Lebesby Man.'

At the head of the fjord lies Ifjord among its pine forests, where an hotel has just been erected to cater for the wants of travellers along 'Road 50.'

Hopseidet

This place lies on the narrow isthmus that joins the Nordkyn Peninsula to the Continent of Europe. At Outer Hop there 'formerly lived many people here and there was a church with three towers'—as it was written in 1694. But even at that date all the glory had departed, and by 1750 it was entirely depopulated.

Hopseidet was reopened before 1799 by a shipwrecked Frenchman who was born in Normandy in 1768. He is said to have fled his country at the Revolution.

There have been schemes for cutting a canal through the 1,200 yards long 'eidet' to obviate the necessity of sailing round stormy Nordkyn peninsula—but the isthmus remains solid land!

For many weeks during the winter of 1944 a Norwegian guard of thirty men was their most advanced outpost to the west. German patrol vessels were then stationed at Honningsvaag and patrolled eastwards to Nordkyn and into Laksefjord. Refugees kept arriving at Hopseidet who dragged their boats on rollers across the isthmus to the Tanafjord side.

Tanafjord

Coastal Lapps lived at Gullholmen, and a chapel was built for them in 1718. A church was consecrated in 1851 at Langnes, farther up the Tana River.

For many years a ferry has bridged the Tana at Seida, but in 1948 a modern bridge was erected a mile farther up, that carries the traffic on Road 50.

Yet two miles higher up is the village of Skipagurra, where the catches of salmon in the mighty Tana are dealt with, and exported to Oslo and world markets.

The last Norwegian village on the right bank of the Tana is Polmak, where Norwegians settled as early as 1790. Here preached the Bishop of (liberated) North Norway exactly three weeks before he gave a sermon from the pulpit in Westminster Abbey on April 9, 1945, on the occasion of the Dano-Norwegian service there to commemorate the fifth year of German occupation of their countries.

Varanger Peninsula

On the Ocean coast here are four main fishing centres—Berlevaag, Kongsfjord, Baatsfjord and Havningberg.

Berlevaag thrived in early days, and legends go that a castle stood on the point of Kjølnes close by. It has a poor harbour and its future is in doubt, since Kongsfjord is more favourably situated.

Vardø

This place had a church in 1307 and was the capital of ancient Finnmark when that province was called Vardøhus. Many references have been made to its history in this volume.

A transit of Venus was to take place on June 3, 1769, and astronomers from many countries were despatched to remote corners of the earth. Denmark found the necessary funds to send Professor Maxmilian Hell, a learned Austrian Jesuit, together with a Hungarian Jesuit, to Vardø, and they took a young theological student, Borchgrevink of Roros, as an assistant. Amtmann Hagerup took passage in the same vessel, which anchored at Vardø October 11, 1768. Before Christmas an observatory had been erected, of timbers plugged with moss.

The Hungarian, by name Sainovics, learnt the Lappish language during the winter and wrote a learned treatise on it to prove that it was one with the Magyar tongue, whilst Borchgrevink collected and dried botanical specimens. But although the weather that winter was exceptionally good there were many complaints at its severity, and as June 3rd approached so did fears increase that their long journey might prove fruitless if the heavens should be blacked-out at the critical period.

The sky was covered in dense clouds between 3 and 6 p.m., but then the sun began to appear. At 8.45 p.m. a gentle south-west breeze swept the clouds aside, and just after 9 the transit began with perfect vision. Then clouds again covered the sun for a long while, and the hours of night (it was midnight sun of course) slipped by. And then about 3 a.m. on June 4, 1769: 'when everything looked black for us and the sun lay behind clouds, a gentle south-east breeze suddenly got up . . . and we were successful in observing the transit of Venus to its close.'

Before he left Pater Hell erected a couple of stone columns at highwater mark at Vardø, so that posterity might measure any alteration in the coastline, and he made an entry to that effect in the Church Register. On June 27, 1769, the astronomers sailed away.

Vardø was given a Royal Charter as a 'town' in 1789 which was forty-four years earlier than that of Vadsø. It still stands on its island (Ø)—though 'the planners' want the town moved across Bussesundet to the mainland.

Vadsø

The road from Vardø runs through ancient Kiberg, and then the island of Ekerrøy, so often mentioned in early history, is passed just before entering Vadsø.

In its young days Vadsø stood with its church on the island now called Kirkeøy, but drifted to the mainland in the seventeenth century, where a new church was built in 1710. A place with little history when compared with ancient Vardø, it did not receive its Royal Charter until 1833. It faces south across Varangerfjord, and lies in less barren surroundings than Vardø and the Arctic Ocean settlements. It is now the administrative capital for all Finnmark.

Bishop Mathias Bonsach Krogh was born here in 1754.

SYDVARANGER

Nyborg

At the head of Varangerfjord this has ever been a 'ting' place. The finest mansion in East Finnmark stood here, and in days gone by parties arrived from almost everywhere around, driving in sledges to celebrate Christmas and Easter. Every possible form of gaiety was indulged in for days on end, and as the military barracks were close by there was always an element of youth about to keep things alive.

Close by lies Karlebotn, where the Lapp market was held, at which the amounts of alcohol consumed ran into astronomical figures.

Neiden

On the river here stands a Greek Orthodox Chapel which, in the days when this part of 'Raftesiden' was Norwegian-Russian 'common-district,' was attached to the church of Boris Gleb near Elvenes. It was used by the Skolte Lapps, whose last remnants have now migrated into Finnish territory. The last service to be held here was in 1916, and the latest burial in the small cemetery in 1927. One solitary Skolte Lapp woman remains (1948), who reverently takes care of the quaint low-pitched timber building with its crude mural paintings.

Kirkenes

The most successful mining concern in Norway was that of Sydvaranger, where immense ore deposits were discovered at Bjørnevatn in 1903, and a company floated for their exploitation in 1906. It took four years before production began, and in 1915 600,000 tons of refined products were exported. That was the peak year, to be followed by coal shortages and the post-war depression. The company was reconstructed in 1927, and then became the largest mining undertaking in all Norway.

The Germans wrecked the mines and plant, but their reconstruction is proceeding. The refining plant was erected at Kirkenes where a fine natural harbour ensures perfect loading conditions. The town has grown up around, but its only history is that of devastation by the Germans.

The Lapp Markets in Finnmark and Troms

From earliest times markets have been held on fixed dates at recognized places, where the nomad Lapps could barter the produce of their reindeer and spoils of their hunting for such articles from more civilized parts as were necessities in their primitive economy.

The first market to receive official sanction was at the head of Varangerfjord, where stood from time immemorial a building known as 'Kongsgammen.' In this shed the Bailiff received

179

payment of taxes from the Lapps in Varanger, and here the pastor from Vadsø preached a sermon once in every year following its official recognition in 1688. On every January 28th there assembled here merchants and peasants from the fjord villages, to meet Lapps from Varanger, Utsjoki and other distant inland districts, Russian Lapps (Skolter) from Pasvik and Neiden, and quite a few traders from Torneaa in Sweden. This Varanger Market was prohibited by royal decree in 1760 but reopened in 1831, to continue to flourish until 1896 when it faded out under competition from the trading-places close by.

Kistrand, Karasjok and Kautokeino each held a 'Lapp-Market' during the eighteenth century, but were completely outclassed by the main Finnmark market at Bossekop that has persisted until our own times. Here at the head of Altafjord a barter trade was operated in very ancient times between the dwellers of the coastal district and those of the mountain tundras. The reason why so many Kvens settled here in the early 1700's was that they had entered Norway by an ancient and well-trodden market-highway.

Amtmann Sommerfeldt thus describes Alta Market in 1798: 'Every February a number of citizens from Torneaa in Sweden come over the mountains with their reindeer bringing bar iron, muskets, scissors, locks, nails and metal utensils, tar, linen, a coarse kind of canvas which the mountain Lapps use for tents, etc., etc. These goods they barter for dried cod, salted salmon and halibut, wool and blankets, skins of reindeer, fox, bear and wolf. The Swedes accept the goods offered without grading them and, since they usually part with their wrought iron at a low figure, this Swedish trade is of great benefit to Finnmark.'

Although the official market was held at Elvebakken until its removal in 1844 to Bossekop, it was ever the latter place that was the meeting-place, and Schnitler wrote in 1744 that Norwegians, Kvens and Lapps who live in the forest and mountains had their fish sheds at Bossekop. It looked like a good-sized village with trading booths and sheds in rows. These were locked up and deserted most of the year, but when market-time approached there was great activity. Loaded vessels entered the harbour, whilst from the hills and forest came the sound of sleigh bells mingled with the cheerful calls of the Lapps as they drove down to the shore. They made a colourful show in their magnificent skin coats with bright coloured caps and glittering finery. The weary reindeer then lay down between the sleighs that were piled high with skins, such game as ptarmigan and 'kvenbutter.' It was a veritable Babel with the three languages—Norwegian, Finnish and Lappish—but all understood one another.

Skibotn Market

The only genuine Lapp-market in Troms was at Skibotn. It had been held three times a year—in November, January and March—from remote times, but was not authorized until 1840. This market played an important role in the economy of North Troms, and was attended by most traders in Tromsø and neighbourhood who bartered their fish to fill their larders with reindeer meat, game and 'kven-butter.' Lapps and Kvens drove in their reindeer sleighs from far away over the Swedish mountains beyond Helliskog and down Skibotndal.

Religious fanaticism at Kautokeino

The Swedes began missionary work among the Lapps at about the same time as Thomas von Westen was preaching in Norwegian Finnmark. They built a church at Kautokeino in 1701 and founded a school there in 1742. When the frontier was adjusted in 1751 Kautokeino was taken over by Norway, but the Norwegians failed to maintain any supervision over the Lapps there, who were left to their own devices until a priest was inducted in 1852.

A Swedish priest named Lestadius initiated a religious revival in Swedish Lappland, and in 1845 the story of the 'Lestadian Revival' in Karesuando reached Kautokeino and had a disturbing influence on the Lapps there. They even eschewed all alcohol, though its consumption on both sides of the frontier was considerable. Three Lapps and three Kvens came with Lestadius' daughter bringing copies of his sermons, so it seems that Lestadius knew of this party's intentions.

The six missionaries returned to Kautokeino in the winter of 1848, and continued the 'revival,' and those Lapps who still kept their heads cool begged most earnestly for a Lappish-speaking priest to be sent up at once to keep in check the fanaticism which would inevitably be the outcome, since Lestadius himself lived too far away to control the consequences of his teachings. The Bishop of Tromsø then paid a visit to Kautokeino and expressed his delight at the 'revival,' and that the Lapp children could read the Bible in their own language, but he did implore the State Church Department to appoint a resident priest as soon as possible. It was two years before one arrived and then it was too late.

The Bishop reported later that the 'revival' had taken on a dangerous aspect, and rumours of unrest in Kautokeino came before the winter snow had hardened sufficiently to make travelling possible. It seems that some of the 'converts' had begun to call themselves 'holy' and 'just,' their belief being that sin existed only in their outer limbs and that to possess the Holy Ghost was all that mattered. They had that and therefore were free from all sin, and felt it to be their purpose in life, as being themselves 'The Father, Son and Holy Ghost,' to exterminate all who did not think as they did.

Hvoslef, the new Lappish-speaking priest, had arrived in April 1852 and quiet appeared to have returned to their troubled minds. But at midnight on November 7th the zealots visited a small group of tents belonging to some 'unconverted,' and these were brutally whipped and tortured. Next morning they went to the store, where the 'innkeeper' and sheriff were living. Their leader called out 'Convert yourself you Devil's sheriff,' and then struck him down, bit his nose just as his dream had indicated he should do, and then stabbed him to death. The priest rushed to the spot and saw the crazy women mishandling the dead 'innkeeper,' but was himself surrounded and whipped, even by small children. They had made up their minds that the devil had to be whipped out of the priest's body, but he survived until a party from another settlement put an end to the disturbances.

When the case was tried at Alta thirty stood trial of whom five were condemned to death but only two were executed. One was given a life sentence because of his extreme youth, and he showed such talent that he was given instruction and assisted Pastor Hvoslef—who later became Bishop of Haalogaland—to revise the translation of the Bible in Lappish.

The Religious Revival at Tromsø, 1854–58

Around 1840 the consumption of spirits in North Norway had reached fantastic proportions, causing great poverty. At that period distillation from potatoes and corn was Norway's premier industry. Disgust with these conditions aroused the more sober section of the public, and, when news of the outbreak of the Crimean War reached Tromsø, people there of all classes turned to religion for comfort and guidance. This rapidly developed into a 'revival' that was fanned by the advent of two Norwegian preachers sent up by the Stavanger Branch of the British and Foreign Bible Society. These two eloquent orators appealed to the emotions, and hence found it easy to arouse their listeners in that isolated corner of Norway. They became the idols of their followers, many of whom believed they were in opposition to the pastors and teachings of the Established Church. There was, however, much superficiality, and therefore the first effect of the teachings did not strike deeper than mundane matters. To foreswear drinking, swearing, dancing and card-playing was the oath that most converts took, though the zealots considered it was sinful to display gold rings or to wear other than black clothes. This movement had some similarity to that promoted by Lestadius in Sweden, which a couple of years previously caused such bestialities to be committed by the Lapp converts at Kautokeino.

The converts were recruited mainly among those less fortunately situated, causing them to condemn the social life and culture of the leading people in the town. Among these latter were the pastors whose influence was weakened, and instead of their guidance and comfort being sought the 'revivalists' turned to tracts and pamphlets of every variety. 'Adiafora' was the name given to 'half-sins' such as dancing, cards, theatres and clubs, and great importance was attached to the suppression of all the 'little sins.' Thereby a yoke was laid on the shoulders of the 'revivalists' that was far different from what Luther had called 'The Freedom of Christianity.' Each and every individual now considered himself to be an authority on theological matters.

Bishop Juell of Haalogaland called his clergy together in 1855 to consider how to combat the spread of sectarian heresies, but the 'revivalists' dubbed them all as a 'crowd of false prophets.' And, to add fuel to the fire, copies of the writings of the Danish philosopher Søren Kierkegaard arrived just then in North Norway, to be misinterpreted and give rise to an agitation against the Church and its rite of baptism.

The people of Tromsø were now divided into two camps bitterly hostile to each other. It was almost a class division, and criticism was levelled against the more cultured throughout 1855.

Then in March 1856 Pastor Lammers left the State Church to be free to found the 'lammersian sect,' and it was not long before the Tromsø rebels had organized their movement on the model of that at Skien.

The State Church at last took counter-action by sending Gislesen, who had been Lammers' eloquent opponent at Skien, up north as Bishop of Haalogaland. So fanatical were some of the dissenters that the Bishop was warned they intended an attempt on his life, and that when the long nights came there would be a repetition of the recent happenings at Kautokeino! Like those poor Lestadian Lapps they believed that Christ and Truth had now taken up abode within their bodies, and they judged without mercy such as did not think as they did—even old friends. One dark evening a street fight took place between the opposing parties, and vindictive intolerance was splitting the people of Tromsø into angels of Heaven and devils of Hell without any moderates to require a Purgatory.

This atmosphere of hatred put an end to the general 'revival' which had made rapid headway in the town until 1855. Social events ceased to be held, even the Musical Society abandoned its *soirées* and travelling artists played to empty houses. For those who had doubts hesitated to attend, and many remained at home for fear of reprisals.

Lammers himself came to Tromsø at Midsummer 1857, having been called for by the dissenters who had previously had to content themselves with casual preachers. He worked for a whole year in Tromsø and preached to packed meeting-houses with persuasive eloquence. His influence was good, and when he one fine day walked into the Bishop's Palace he found the door wide open. The acute bitterness and mutual hatred subsided before Lammers went south in April 1858. Bishop Gislesen had triumphed, and Lammers circulated to his flock an admission of the errors of his teachings when he re-entered the State Church in 1860.

Trading Relations with the White Sea Russians

A vital factor in the life of Finnmark throughout the nineteenth century was the trade with Russian White Sea ports. As early as 1773 Finnmark was largely provisioned with rye flour from Russia, despite the fact that such trade was prohibited. The Napoleonic Wars put many obstacles in the way, but after 1811 Russian trade was carried on as far south as Nordland Province, and it was that trade which kept Finnmark alive through the years of want. It was revived when the war ended, and was extended in 1818 to the harbours in what is now the Province of Troms. In 1839 a Norwegian decree allowed Russians to buy fish in Vesteraalen, and this permit was extended in 1866 to cover Lofoten ports as well.

We have a description of what Russian trade meant in 1830 in the following contemporary account: 'Russian trade is of inestimable value to the Province, and therefore Russians are always welcome guests whom both traders and the general public vie with one another to entice to their fjords. When the Russian vessels appear in the Spring new life and activity awake everywhere in Finnmark. The articles they bring are almost exclusively necessities, and usually of excellent quality. All sorts of cereals, especially coarse-ground rye flour, wheaten flour, oats and millet-seed, peas, flax, hemp, canvas and linen, rope work, tar, tallow, soap, syrup, wax and honey, etc.' . . . They screwed up the barter value of flour when there was a shortage, but the 'innkeepers' usually managed to regulate the barter value of fish so as to prevent cereals soaring to impossible figures.

The Russians who carried on the trade with Finnmark were mainly peasants from the Province of Archangel and were called 'Pomorer,' a word that means 'those who live near the sea.' They bought most of their flour from the rich cornlands around Archangel which was floated down the River Dvina. In early days they imported Norwegian fish under the pretext that it was their own catch. But by three Russian Decrees between 1851 and 1862 all citizens and peasants in the districts of Kem, Onega and Archangel had the right to freely export their own products to Norway and to import fishery products under a low tariff. The Russian trade was looked upon with favour by both the Norwegian and Russian Governments, perhaps, however, more so by the former.

The background for this 'pomor' trade from the Russian point of view was the enormous demand for fish during church 'fasts.' What Finnmark had lost in trade with the Roman Catholic countries in Europe she recovered to a great extent in Greek-Orthodox Russia. In the days of the Czars there were numerous 'fasts,' including the forty days of Lent, 'Peter-Paul's fast, the fast of 'Our Lady,' and the Christmas fast which endured for forty days prior to Christmas Eve. There were also the Wednesday and Friday fasts, in addition to fixed Saints days, all these 'fasts' being strictly observed by the Russians of those times.

The 'skippers' of the Russian vessels were superior in every respect to their crews and were regarded as friends by the Norwegian traders. It was customary for the young sons of the latter to live in the homes of the 'skippers' for a year or more to learn the language. A natural consequence of this connection was that houses in Finnmark were often graced by artistic pieces of Russian workmanship, but Hitler's devastation of Finnmark has destroyed most of these pleasant reminders of the happy relations that used to exist between the two peoples. There are still a few 'finnmarkinger' living who remember that strange blending of the two national tongues called 'russenorsk,' in which all dealings and social converse was carried on. The isolated Arctic Ocean fishing villages were one and all visited by the 'Pomorer,' and that there would come a time when an 'iron curtain' would put an end to the genuine friendships existing between skippers, crews and residents was unthinkable.

When the First World War broke out Russian trade was flourishing, and it would undoubtedly have developed, though perhaps on other lines, if it could have continued in peace. A mutually beneficial trade ceased abruptly when the Russian Revolution of 1917–18 put an end to all private enterprise. The happy days of 'Pomor' trading in Finnmark had passed away.

Frontier Questions with Russia and Finland

As late as 1809 Norway had no agreed frontier with Russia. It flowed out in the 'common districts' of Neiden, Pasvik, Peisen and Enare. With the surrender of Finland to Russia by Sweden at the Treaty of Frederikshamn in 1809—further confirmed by the demarcation Act of 1810—Russia marched in to Sweden's former position as Norway's neighbour along all the inland limits of Finnmark Province.

Although the Treaty of Frederikshamn did not give Russia any further rights in the ancient Norwegian-Russian 'common districts,' it weakened Norway's influence among the Lapps living within them. The Skolte (Russian) Lapps increased their efforts to gain control in these districts, and this rendered it a matter of urgency for the Norwegian Government to effect an exchange with Russia so as to obtain a delimited frontier. The Governor of East Finnmark wrote: 'The common-districts are the bones of contention which cause disputes between subjects of the two kingdoms. As long as this stretch of territory continues to be 'common' the strife between them will continue.'

The Frontier Commissions of the two countries met in 1825, and the resulting Convention was well received in both Norway and Russia. It was signed in St. Petersburg on May 2, 1826, and the delimitation of the whole frontier was completed in 1827.

This Agreement, however, was later the subject of criticism, especially from Russians and Finns, and the Russian Commissioner was accused of accepting bribes from Norway. Actually the gift consisted of a gold case studded with diamonds, and the charge was one of sheer malice. Finland complained that no representative of the Grand Duchy had been summoned to the negotiations, and that some of her 'ancient economic rights' were surrendered by the Convention. At long last Finnmark Province had got a delimited frontier, and age-old disputes as to its correct limits were settled for all time, and in a manner with which Norway had every reason to be satisfied.

Just prior to the Crimean War, however, there were indications that Russia had aggressive designs at Finnmark's expense.

On September 5, 1851, Palmerston wrote to the British Minister in Stockholm: 'I have to instruct you strongly to dissuade the Swedish Government from making to Russia any cession of territory in that quarter (Finnmark). Such cession would only serve as a foundation for further encroachments, and afford a basis of a Naval Station commanding the coast of Norway.

In 1852, in consequence of disputes over Finnish grazing rights, the relations between Russia and Norway cooled, and the Russians closed a part of the frontier. This was regarded as an *acte peu amicale*.

On January 30, 1854, the British Chargé d'Affaires at Stockholm wrote to Lord Clarendon that the head of the Swedish Foreign Office had expressed a fear that Russia wanted to seize some portion of Finnmark where harbours never froze, and mentioned Varangerfjord. On April 27, 1854, the Admiralty replied to Clarendon: '. . . it is most important to uphold in the strongest manner any protest which Sweden may make against the appropriation of Varanger Bay by Russia.'

Palmerston's attention to possible danger in Northern Norway was aroused by a despatch of May 23, 1855, from J. R. Crowe (then Consul-General at Christiania, but previously Vice-Consul, Hammerfest) in which he urged that if any part of Finnmark fell into Russian hands it would be a 'blow to the chief cornerstone of Norwegian independence' which it was a vital British interest to prevent. On this Palmerston remarked: 'It would be desirable to initiate negotiations with the King of Sweden and Norway to induce him to undertake the duty of not conceding to Russia either fishing or grazing rights or territory without the consent of Great Britain. Such a treaty would give him permanent assistance.' Next day the draft of a Pact of Guarantee was prepared, which was laid before King Oscar. The Treaty was signed on November 21, 1855, and has since been known to Norwegian historians as *The November Treaty*. This treaty received an enthusiastic welcome from the leading English newspapers. It provided a guarantee of military assistance by land and sea to co-operate with the Swedish-Norwegian forces in opposition to any Russian demands or aggression.

The check to Russian advance to the north-west was 'The November Treaty.'

When the Bobrikoff regime was established in Finland at the close of the last century, it was believed in Scandinavia to be the first step in a planned expansion towards the Atlantic at the cost of Sweden and Norway. Russian saw-sharpeners, said to be disguised Russian officers, were wandering about northern Scandinavia. At the turn of the century Russian military circles regarded expansion to the Atlantic through northern Scandinavia as something quite natural, but no elaborated plan came to light.

However, the Japanese victory over Russia in 1904 put an end for many years to Imperialist Russian pretensions.

Norway acquired sovereign independence in 1905, at a time when the world appeared set for a long period of peace. For nearly a century the *Pax Britannica* had kept the 'Seven Seas' clear for the passage of ships of every nation upon their lawful occasions. The measure of freedom of the individual and the contentment (some called it *pathetic* contentment) of the masses, in even the most backward countries, were on a scale undreamed of in most of the world today.

Those of us who can remember 1905 may be forgiven for considering it to have been the 'Golden Age.'

PART IX

THE TWENTIETH CENTURY

JUST as in the rest of the world, more history was made in North Norway during the twentieth century than throughout all the aeons of time that have elapsed since the Ice Age. We are too near the actual events for history to pass judgment upon them, so only a brief summary of a few major incidents will be given in this chapter.

What dreams did Kaiser Wilhelm II indulge in when his yacht *Hohenzollern* lay anchored on so many occasions at Digermulen? We know that there he used to glory in the scenery of his favourite Raftsund and its enchanting little Trollfjord. Surely he dreamt of the time when all the world should lay at his feet, would have gloated at the vision of himself as Lord of his cherished Norway, and of how he would spend long weeks in his old age among its lovely mountains and fjords? His destiny, however, led him to eke out his misspent life as an exile on the green cloth of the billiard table that is Holland.

When at Digermulen the Kaiser would have sensed his iron ore ships passing almost under the stern of the anchored *Hohenzollern*, plimsoll mark awash with their ladings for his munition factories in Westphalia.

It is one of the greatest tragedies of history that the iron ore mountains in Swedish Lappland were ever discovered. That perhaps could not have been avoided, but when their exploitation passed from the British concessionaires into 'neutral' hands, there was nothing to prevent their providing the war potential for an aggressive Germany to wage those two world wars, that sometimes appear to have set civilization back 1,500 years to the time of Attila. Certain it is that, without the flow of the raw material for destruction through Narvik, neither war would have attained such gigantic proportions. All there has been on the credit side was an amassing of wealth in neutral Sweden, that has enabled that country to raise its standard of living to extravagant heights and to institute what is perhaps the finest welfare service in the world. Narvik itself progressed for some forty years—only to be destroyed by the finished products of the very raw material that had passed along its railway and from its quays between and during both World Wars.

The First World War

When in 1914 those ore shipments continued to pass down the coast of Norway in German bottoms, secure in the channels of the 'Inner Lead' and Norwegian territorial waters, Britain made feeble efforts to stop the traffic without infringing Norway's neutrality. The auxiliary cruiser H.M.S. *India*, that had once been the pride of the P. and O. fleet, was sunk by torpedo in the Vestfjord, and most churchyards in that vicinity now contain graves of members of its crew—notably Bodø and Kabelvaag.

Russia required the assistance of her allies in the 1914 war (just as in that of 1941) to keep her armies in the field, and frantic efforts were made to construct a railway to an ice free port in Murmansk. British contractors came up against the inefficiency (or worse) of Russian bureaucrats, and completion of the railway was disastrously delayed. The munition factories of Russia were not at that time sufficiently developed to manufacture certain instruments of precision, so these had to be got across to her by some means. Sweden would not permit her neutrality to be 'stretched' to admit of this—indeed at one period the attitude of the Swedish Government to the Allies was such that that wise old political leader Hjalmar Branting came over to England specially to inform the British authorities that, if his country was swept by Stockholm into war on the side of Germany, he would raise a revolution in Gothenburg within twenty-four hours. So these delicate precision instruments such as fuses, etc., were shipped to Lyngen, whence horse-sleighs transported them through 'the Finnish Wedge' to the system of Russian (Finnish) railways. The neutrality of Norway was 'stretched' to enable these vital munitions to pass through the thirty odd miles of its territory up the Skibotn valley, and thus circumvent neutral Sweden.

Three Swedes acting as German agents were then sent up north to wreck this undertaking. The vigilance of the Norwegian police, however, prevented them carrying out their intentions. In their baggage were found sticks of dynamite in tins labelled 'Asparagus,' several large pencils each of which contained a beautiful piece of glass-blowing that was actually a delay-action incendiary bomb, and, worst of all, innocent-looking cubes of white sugar in plain cardboard boxes. Each cube had a small glass tube within it that was invisible to the naked eye, the contents of which were 'bacilli' that would decimate the horses with fatal diseases such as anthrax and glanders.

The above all happened in the winter of 1916–17, after which the Revolution in Russia ended any contribution by its Army to the war effort of the Allies. British interest in North Norway ceased, except for the purchase of its fish and fish products to prevent their weakening our blockade of Germany via the safety route through Norwegian territorial waters. Enormous sums were expended in North Norway for this purpose—and not a little of the fish thus bought had to be thrown into the sea, for lack of available transport to a friendly country.

The 1914–18 war left no scars upon Norway, except those of the graves of British sailors. Indeed Norway flourished under its neutrality, except of course for the heavy toll taken by German submarines of its merchant sailors all over the 'Seven Seas.'

Between the Wars

The granting to Norway at Versailles in 1920 of a limited sovereignty over Spitsbergen (Svalbard) increased Norwegian interest in the coal deposits there, and Tromsø did a brisk trade with it during the periods of open water. But British interest in North Norway between the wars was largely confined to the tourists and to iron ore, except for the eternal disputes over the entry of British trawlers into territorial waters, and what definition should be accepted of the term 'territorial waters.' Germany had other ideas in the 1930's, and sent General von Blomberg on a tour up there. It now seems strange that his visit was not regarded as a warning of German intentions in the far north, and that precautions were not taken.

The Second World War

There were early indications that the peace with which North Norway had been blessed through more than a century would soon be broken, and the 'Finnish Winter War' with Russia compelled Norway to establish a neutrality guard along her Pasvik frontier. The Finns were quickly evicted by Russia from the former Russian territory that Versailles granted them in 1920, and Norway once again had a common frontier with a belligerent Russia.

German iron ore ships were passing down the 'Inner Lead' during the winter of 1939–40 under the security of Norwegian neutrality, which Britain did not see fit to infringe. Not so Germany, however, and some British ore ships were torpedoed within territorial waters. When questioned in the Storting the Norwegian Foreign Minister queried whether torpedoes or mines had caused the series of disasters, though no sailors ever had the slightest doubt. Their sympathy and indignation were expressed in a touching manner when the express coastal steamers passed over the spot where a British ship had recently been sunk. Engines were stopped and a wreath cast upon the waters whilst all heads were bowed. These ore ships went down like stones owing to the nature of their cargo, and survivors were rare.

The *Altmark*, with its imprisoned British merchant sailors collected in the South Atlantic, entered the 'Inner Lead' in North Norway. Fortunately the captain of a small British steamer passed her just as he was turning into Trondheimsfjord, and gave the first and only warning from Norway of her presence on its coast. Without this chance meeting in the 'Inner Lead,' London would never have known of the *Altmark's* presence, since no coast-watching reports were—even clandestinely—passed to the British authorities by Norwegians. There had been no breaches of neutrality whatsoever on the part of the Norwegian Government to justify German occupation of Norway on April 9, 1940.

It was with the seizure of Narvik on April 9, 1940, that North Norway was dragged into the war, and there, in the grey dawning, two ancient coastal defence vessels of her navy put up a hopeless yet magnificent gesture of defiance. Two actions by the British Navy ensued, the second of which left Narvik Harbour filled with sunken wrecks, and the banks of Rombaksfjord nearby with battered German destroyers that had run ashore to save life. There followed an improvised campaign by Norwegian, French, British and Polish forces to evict the German garrison from Narvik, the aftermath of which can be seen in the cemeteries there. Much of the inner story of those days in April and May 1940 has been vividly described in that fascinating book *The Mountains Wait* by Theodor Broch, who was Mayor of Narvik at that time.

All this while a battalion of the Scots Guards, with Norwegian support, had been fighting a rearguard action up the centre of Nordland Province along Road 50. Hemnes was the one spot where a stand might have been made, since the road north from Mosjøen ceased at Elsfjord and a ferry journey of nine miles was essential till Hemnes was reached, whence the road once more carried on to the north. It might have been only a question of securing the ferry and all craft at the Hemnes end before the enemy arrived, but a considerable force of Germans, having been rigged up in Norwegian uniforms, were shipped in a coastal steamer at Trondheim. The transmission of the intelligence concerning this ruse was bungled, and the steamer landed its troops at Hemnes only a short while before H.M.S. *Liverpool* arrived (just too late) on the scene to deal with the situation. The presence of this British force gave the Germans some excuse for bombing the towns of Fauske and Bodø, from which latter port the Scots Guards embarked for England.

Harstad and Tromsø were hives of activity during the first two months of Norway's war, but all was over in the first week of June following the collapse on the Franco-Belgian front. The King, his Government and all non-Norwegian forces took ship for England, running the gauntlet of the German Navy which took a heavy toll.

The hobnailed boots of the German soldier were now trampling down everything in North Norway. General Dietl's army took over Finnmark, where almost every dwelling had Norway's enemies billeted in great numbers.

Road 50, and the railway under construction through Nordland (especially in the district of Salten) became the scenes of unspeakable barbarity inflicted by their German guards upon the numerous Slav prisoners-of-war, doing forced labour through the bitter winter cold, scantily clothed and almost without food. The local inhabitants were witnesses to cruelty in many a hideous form, and the mass graves by the roadside will ever remain as startling evidences of man's inhumanity to man.

The first fishing vessel from North Norway to arrive in the Shetlands sailed from Vesteraalen in January 1941 loaded with patriots. Many others followed in their train, a few of whom, alas, never saw land again.

On March 4, 1941, the first commando raid on enemy occupied territory was made on four fishing ports in the Lofotens, returning the same day to Scotland with all the Norwegian youth they could find space for. The reprisals taken gave the Norwegian people as a whole their first real insight into the bestiality of the Gestapo, their own reaction being an upsurge of the Resistance Movement. It was stated in official circles in London that had there been no other dividend from the raid than the papers snatched up in the office of the German Harbourmaster at Svolvaer, the expedition was yet justified a thousandfold.

A Norwegian destroyer called at Øksfjord in Finnmark in April 1941, but unfortunately returned without volunteers.

Another landing was effected on December 26, 1941, at Reine in the Outer Lofotens. The disaster at Pearl Harbour about a fortnight previously, however, rendered it tactically necessary to withdraw from the Lofotens after forty-eight hours there, instead of as intended remaining all winter to harry the iron ore traffic from Narvik and to hamstring the German Army on the Finland front. Had this operation been carried through it might have proved a valuable precursor to 'Operation Jupiter,' which was Mr. Churchill's pet scheme for seizing North Norway and making contact with Russia. Once again numbers of local inhabitants were brought back to Scotland, to spare them the reprisals which had been a consequence of the previous raid.

It seems to be established beyond doubt that it was these early raids upon the Norwegian coast that gave Hitler his 'intuition' that the Western Powers would try to reconquer Europe via Norway, and caused him to fritter away considerable man-power and war effort in an intensive fortification of much of Norway's coastline.

The Resistance Movement worked feverishly all over North Norway, one sad incident being the betrayal of a group in the Majavattn District of Helgeland, who were creating dumps of sabotage material sent out to the Bindal area from Britain. Fifteen young men from that sparsely populated district were executed for their participation, and the grief occasioned there was acute. The leader was a brave young Swede, who was later killed in that district and now lies buried in Mosjøen churchyard, where his grave is an object of veneration by all Helgeland.

After Germany had literally driven Russia into Britain's camp in the summer of 1941 the sea route to Murmansk had to be kept open, as had been the case a quarter of a century earlier. The 'Murmansk Convoys' were among the most arduous of the manifold duties of the British Royal and Merchant navies—and off the coast of Finnmark were sacrificed the lives of hundreds of seamen of the Western Powers. German planes from Bardufoss aerodrome, and submarines from bases in North Norway, made the narrow waters between Norway's coast and the edge of the polar ice a veritable inferno.

It was also off the coast of Finnmark that the *Scharnhorst* was sunk. When the commanding British Admiral was raised to the peerage for this battle, he chose for his title 'Lord Fraser of North Cape,' thus utilizing a name that had been given to that promontory by a former British commander, Richard Chancellor, in 1553.

The *Tirpitz* lay wounded in Kaafjord, Alta, and was about to sail after temporary repairs, when British midget submarines made their heroic and successful attack. The moment for this was chosen in consequence of radio messages from a secret transmitter on the spot, that was serviced by young Norwegians in constant danger of their lives. The *Tirpitz* eventually limped her way to Tromsø, where the R.A.F. made an all-out attack, as a result of which she now lies there bottom up and with many skeletons of her crew imprisoned within her rusting hull.

In the autumn of 1944 the German Army in Finland was forced to retreat through Finnmark. The Russians followed so close on their heels that German devastation in East Finnmark could not be the 100 per cent they had intended. The Arctic Ocean villages of Havningberg and Baatsfjord suffered no destruction whatever, whilst Vardø, Vadsø and Kirkenes each had a few houses left. Everything went up in flames throughout West Finnmark, and in Troms as far as Lyngen, since General Rendulic decided to scorch the earth and delay a Russian advance—which as a matter of fact did not extend beyond the Tana River.

Norwegian Civil Servants were re-established in East Finnmark as soon as the Germans had evacuated, but the difficulties were immense since dwellings were almost non-existent and many local Norwegians had evaded the compulsory evacuation to the south by hiding away in caves, in turf huts and under upturned boats. Norwegian fishing vessels made nightly journeys into 'no-man's-land' to rescue these 'huleboer' (cave-dwellers), but vigilance was necessary since German naval craft remained based on Honningsvaag until the final liberation in May. These enemy craft made occasional trips eastwards when they relentlessly burnt all shelters, and any Norwegians caught were forcibly evacuated with nothing but the clothes they were wearing.

News was brought to Gamvik from Sørøya that 1,000 huleboer remained on that large island opposite Hammerfest. Their situation was desperate and they needed assistance urgently. Three fishing cutters made their way there through the darkness, and evacuated 200 of them to Baatsfjord, but the problem was too big for East Finnmark to tackle. The Norwegian doctor flew to

London from Kirkenes, and the Admiralty agreed to detach four destroyers from a Murmansk convoy to take off 500 Sørøya huleboer on January 15, 1945. A fortnight later these were landed in Glasgow—so visitors to the lonely islands in the Norwegian Arctic will find residents there who know something of Scotland and the English language.

There was much bitterness and indignation among the evacuees who were driven out of Finnmark and north Troms during the severe winter cold. They could not understand why the supreme command of the Western Allies could not spare a few troops to mop up the German retaining force, whose morale they knew to be at a very low ebb. It is to be hoped they now realize that had a landing been made in perhaps Troms, there would have been more scorched earth south of that landing, and the sufferings of Norway might have been vastly increased. All visitors to Finnmark will, however, remember that they are among a people who have suffered as a whole more at the hands of the enemy than have any other Scandinavians.

When 'Liberation' came in May 1945 the desire of nearly all 'Finnmarkinger' was to get home again as quickly as possible. Although they had been enjoying amenities in the south of Norway such as they had never experienced in their own distant province, yet it was Home they were determined to return to. The rebuilding of their homes is proving a lengthy undertaking since difficulties of weather, labour and transport are immense— but Finnmark is rising from its ashes.

The abundance of fish in the Arctic Ocean will ever attract folk to its bleak and distant shores. These people now man the north-eastern outpost of our civilization, and here also hangs 'The Iron Curtain,' along the sole frontier with Russia among the countries that have so far signed the Atlantic Pact.

Any winged objects that fly straight as an arrow would pass over Finnmark on their route from the Kremlin to the teeming cities of the New World.

BIBLIOGRAPHY

In English

Acerbi, J.: *Travels to the North Cape*, 1798–99 (London, 1802).
Brooke, A. de Capell: *A Winter in Lapland and Sweden* (1827); *Travels to the North Cape* (London, 1823).
Buch, Leopold von: *Travels in Norway and Lapland* (London, 1813).
Du Chaillu, Paul: *Land of the Midnight Sun* (London, 1881).
Metcalfe, Rev. Frederick: *The Oxonian in Norway* (1856).

In Norwegian

Amtmennenes femaarsberetninger om rikets tiltstand.
Coldevin, Axel: *Jordegods og Storgaarder i Nord-Norge* (*Trondheim*, 1943).
Haalogalands Aarbøker.
Hagemann, A.: *Engelskmanden under Finmarken* (Kristiania, 1891).
Heber Gustav: *Haalogalands Urtid og Fortid* (Oslo, 1934).
Helland, A: *Norges Land og Folk.*
Johnsen, Oscar Albert: *Finmarkens politiske Historie* (Kra, 1923).
Kraft, J.: *Topographisk-statistisk Beskrivelse* (Kristiania, 1835).
Muribø, Elias: *Petter Dass* (Trondheim, 1947).
Nielsen, Yngvar: *Det halve Kongerike* (Kristiania, 1911).
Stambanen gjennom Nord-Norge (Bodø, 1949).
Wiberg, Christian Koren: *Helene Duncan* (Kristiania, 1919).
Ytreberg, N. A.: *Nordlandske Handelsteder* (Trondheim, 1941).
   Handelsteder i Finnmark (Trondheim, 1942).
   Tromsø Bys Historie (Oslo, 1946).

In Landsmaal

Eidnes, Hans: *Haalogalands Historie* (Trondheim, 1943).

The German Occupation

Broch, Theodor: *The Mountains Wait* (London, 1943).
Fjellbu, Bishop Arne: *Minner fra Krigsaarene* (Oslo, 1946).
Finnmark i Flammer (Kragerø, 1950).
Fleischer, General: *Efterlatte Papirer* (Tønsberg, 1947).
Markusson, Andreas: *Den siste Skanse* (Oslo, 1945).
Norges Sjøkrig (Bergen, 1947).
Øya i Ingenmannsland (Sørøya) (Oslo, 1946).

INDEX

GEORGE ALLEN & UNWIN LTD
LONDON: 40 MUSEUM STREET, W.C.1
CAPE TOWN: 58–60 LONG STREET
SYDNEY, N.S.W.: 55 YORK STREET
TORONTO: 91 WELLINGTON STREET WEST
CALCUTTA: 17 CENTRAL AVE., P.O. DHARAMTALA
BOMBAY: 15 GRAHAM ROAD, BALLARD ESTATE
WELLINGTON, N.Z.: 8 KINGS CRESCENT, LOWER HUTT

THE KON-TIKI EXPEDITION

by THOR HEYERDAHL

Demy 8vo. 12s. 6d. *net*

This famous account of the amazing voyage of the Kon-Tiki raft is the finest adventure story of our time.

"The record of this astonishing voyage is one of the most remarkable, exciting and strange stories of travel ever written. Crossing an ocean on a raft is very different from crossing it in any other craft. You are, for one thing, far more intimate with the sea. You are practically *in* it all the time, and the oddest things can, and do, happen. . . . The *Kon-Tiki* was unique (was, alas, for she split on a coral reef) among sea-going vessels. Her story will be a new classic in this kind. Mr. Heyerdahl's frank, original and engaging personality comes out in his vigorous writing. He has been so well served by his translator (Mr. F. H. Lyon) that the reader does not notice that he is reading a translation."

C. V. WEDGWOOD in *The Bookman*

"The expedition has produced the most fascinating travel book published in this country in many years. . . . But I think their most important discovery was the pleasure of adventure undertaken against the best possible professional advice."

FREDERICK LAWS in *News Chronicle*

"This exhilarating exploit proves that the Polynesians could have come from Peru—not that they did; and one would like to know whether Mr. Heyerdahl has rallied any experts to his theory. I have never read a more tonic story of adventure; it reads like a schoolboy's daydream."

RAYMOND MORTIMER in *Sunday Times*

"Mr. Heyerdahl in easy-flowing style, relates a string of apparent miracles."

OLIVER WARNER in *Time and Tide*

KON-TIKI AND I

by ERIK HESSELBERG

Demy 4to. 10s. 6d. *net*

No one who has enjoyed *The Kon-Tiki Expedition* can afford to miss this book. Erik Hesselberg was the navigator member of the *Kon-Tiki's* crew.
In this light-hearted book Hesselberg tells the story—mainly in delightful pen drawings. His pen has caught vivid impressions of the life at sea and the unbelievably cramped quarters of the tiny bamboo cabin.

AMERICAN INDIANS IN THE PACIFIC

by THOR HEYERDAHL

In preparation

In this book Thor Heyerdahl sets out in detail the facts supporting his theory of Polynesian origins in early America.

FOURTEEN MEN

by ARTHUR SCHOLES

Demy 8vo. 15*s. net*

This is the story of the Australian Antarctic Expedition to Heard Island, a fragment of land, separated from Australia by 2,500 miles of the wildest and loneliest seas in the world, and so minute that it is not to be found on any but the largest maps.

On November 28, 1947, with thirteen companions, the author set out by landing ship from Fremantle and, after a long and violent passage and a hazardous landing, set up their camp among the sea-elephants, penguins, shags and other creatures of the Antarctic wastes. There they were isolated for fifteen months, swept from time to time by the blizzards and hurricanes that roared in from the empty wastes of water which completely circled the globe on either hand. Their only contact with the outside world was by radio. Their object was to establish a weather station, to study cosmic rays, magnetic observations, and to make tidal records, and glaciological and geological surveys.

Arthur Scholes, who was born in Cheshire and has recently lectured on the expedition to enthralled audiences up and down this country, presents us with a vivid picture of this part of the world, and tells an intimate story of how so small and isolated a group of men made their lives there tolerable. The many illustrations are from the official photographer, Alan Campbell-Drury, a companion at Heard Island.

I'LL FLY NO MORE

by URSULA BARNETT POTTER

Demy 8vo. 18*s. net*

The writer has quite literally flown the length and breadth of Africa—not as a dozing passenger in a giant multi-engined aircraft but as navigator for her husband in a small private aeroplane with one engine. Thrice they have flown between South Africa and Europe—on one journey accompanied by their two young children. One of the flights she describes was from the Atlantic coast of Africa across the Congo to the Great Lakes—that is, over more than a thousand miles of solid forest, above the land of the pygmies and through the Kivu volcanoes and the Mountains of the Moon.

The story, which is told in diary form, has many passages of vivid description in which the fears and perils of such journeying are well portrayed—the crossing of the Angola mountains, a forced landing on a forest airstrip alongside the River Congo almost on the equator, and being caught in a thunderstorm above the battlefields of the Western Desert.

She reveals herself as gay, good humoured and adventurous and although she has said that she will 'fly no more,' there is a note of doubt in the declaration.

GEORGE ALLEN & UNWIN LTD

THANK YOU FOR RETURNING YOUR BOOKS ON TIME!

NORTH NORWAY

18

10   12   14   16

70

69

VESTERAALEN

Malangen

Senja

TRO

Bardu

Harstad

68

LOFOTEN

Svolvær

Ofotfj

Narvik

Tysfj

Vestfj

S
A
L
T
E
N

67

NORDLAND

Bodö

Gildeskadl

Artic Circle

66

Dönna

Mo i Rana

Alstahaug

H
E
L
G
E
L
A
N
D

Vega

Mosjöen

Brönnöysund

65

Bindål

0 20 40 60 80 100   150 km